AF413445

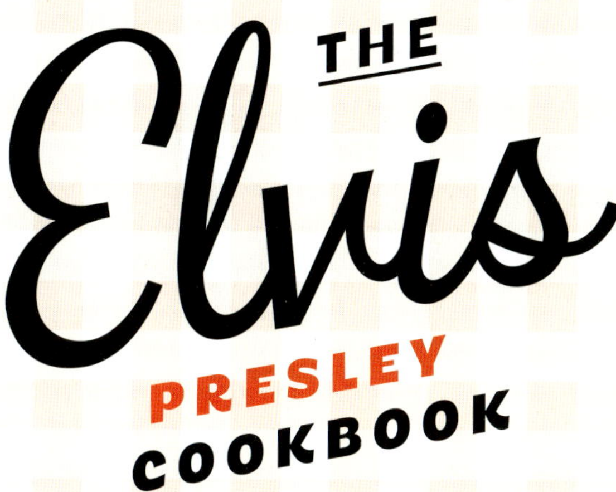

FUN FACTS AND SIMPLE SOUTHERN COMFORT RECIPES FIT FOR A KING

ELIZABETH MCKEON, RALPH GEVIRTZ, AND JULIE BANDY

ELVIS'S HAIR WAS JUST ONE ELEMENT IN HIS NATURAL
GOOD LOOKS; HERE HE IS GETTING IT STYLED.

The Elvis Presley Cookbook

Copyright © 1992 Elizabeth McKeon, Ralph Gevirtz, Julie Bandy

Previously published as *Fit for a King*.

All rights reserved. No portion of this book may be reproduced, stored in a retrieval system, or transmitted in any form or by any means—electronic, mechanical, photocopy, recording, scanning, or other—except for brief quotations in critical reviews or articles, without the prior written permission of the publisher.

Published by Harper Celebrate, an imprint of HarperCollins Focus LLC.

Any internet addresses, phone numbers, or company or product information printed in this book are offered as a resource and are not intended in any way to be or to imply an endorsement by Harper Celebrate, nor does Harper Celebrate vouch for the existence, content, or services of these sites, phone numbers, companies, or products beyond the life of this book.

Without limiting the exclusive rights of any author, contributor or the publisher of this publication, any unauthorized use of this publication to train generative artificial intelligence (AI) technologies is expressly prohibited. HarperCollins also exercise their rights under Article 4(3) of the Digital Single Market Directive 2019/790 and expressly reserve this publication from the text and data mining exception.

Art direction and cover design: Tiffany Forrester
Front cover photography: Michael Ochs Archives / Stringer via Getty Images
Back cover photography: © StockFood / Harrison, Michael S.; © StockFood / Keller & Keller Photography; © ricka_kinamoto / Adobe Stock
Additional photography credits listed at the back of the book.
Interior design: Kristen Sasamoto

ISBN 978-1-4002-56280 (HC)

Printed in India
26 27 28 29 30 REP 5 4 3 2 1

Contents

TAKING A COFFEE BREAK ON
THE SET OF *LOVING YOU*

APPETIZERS

SOUPS AND SALADS

AUDITIONING FOR *LOVE ME TENDER*

TALKING WITH FANS OUTSIDE THE
GATES OF GRACELAND

EATING ONE OF HIS FAVORITE
FOODS: A CHEESEBURGER

ELVIS, WHO USUALLY DRANK MILK,
TAKING TIME OUT FOR TEA

Foreword

In the spring of 1963, my cousin was working for Elvis Presley at his Bel Air home on Perugia Way. She had heard there was an opening for a cook's position and told me of the opportunity. I met with Elvis, and on May 17, 1963, I went to work for him.

Initially I was quite nervous, but I was soon put at ease by Elvis's warm charm and great sense of humor.

Many exciting events took place during the time I cooked for Elvis. One was when The Beatles visited during their US tour in August 1965. I prepared a midnight supper that included broiled chicken livers wrapped in bacon, sweet-and-sour meatballs, deviled eggs, fresh cracked crab, fruit, and a platter of assorted cold cuts and cheeses.

In September 1965, Elvis moved to Rocca Way, near the Bel Air Hotel. Like the other places Elvis lived, his fans camped out near the front gates just to catch a glimpse of him. When the weather was warm, he would send out glasses of cold lemonade and iced tea.

In the spring of 1967, when it was announced that Elvis and Priscilla would marry, I went to the Palm Springs house to prepare for the May 1 wedding. The menu for the guests was turkey with stuffing and gravy, string beans, and stuffed tomatoes. And of course there was the six-tiered wedding cake decorated with white pearls and red hearts. For "his boys," Elvis had me cook up a batch of spaghetti with French bread.

In October of that year, Elvis asked me to accompany him to Sedona, Arizona, where he was making the Western film *Stay Away, Joe*. During the time we were on location, I prepared many of Elvis's

Introduction

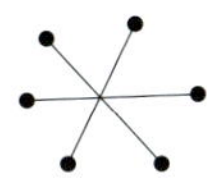

Mention Elvis, and most everyone knows who you are talking about. Mention "The King," and the response is generally the same. It is evident, from all that has ever been said or written about Elvis Presley, that he was, and is, a legend.

In July of 1953, Elvis recorded "My Happiness" and "That's When Your Heartache Begins" at the Memphis Recording Studio, later known as Sun Studio. That summer was just the beginning of a career that would span three decades.

Aside from all the fame, fortune, and recognition that Elvis achieved during his lifetime, he never once forgot where he came from and the values instilled in him by his Southern upbringing.

Born in East Tupelo, Mississippi, he moved with his family to Memphis, Tennessee, when he was thirteen years old. From that moment on, Elvis made Memphis his home. At the age of twenty-two, he bought Graceland, a traditional Southern mansion. In the evenings, Elvis would stroll down to the front gates to talk with his fans. His charming, warm hospitality was neither compromised nor abandoned by his sudden wealth and popularity.

He shared with others, especially with family and friends, who were most important to him. For Elvis it was not uncommon to have them over for dinner. They would gather around the formal dining room to share in a simple meal together. Often prepared were a variety of dishes, many like the ones he enjoyed as a young boy.

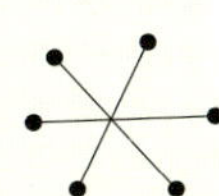

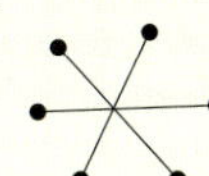

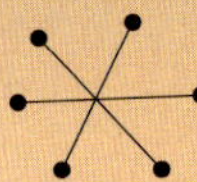

Here now is a collection of recipes popular during the time Elvis was living at Graceland. Some are from Alvena Roy, his longtime cook. Other recipes are for foods he ate regularly, and yet others are for foods he likely served the many guests at his generous table. With them, we hope that you too will create traditional, wholesome, home-cooked meals for your family and friends and that you will enjoy the same warmth in your home as Elvis did at Graceland.

—*Elizabeth McKeon, Ralph Gevirtz, and Julie Bandy*

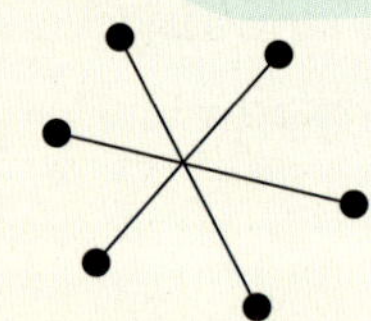

Elvis always considered Graceland and Memphis his home. His friends and family were there: the people he grew up with, went to church and school with. He never thought of leaving and only lived in Hollywood while he was working. He never considered moving to California permanently.

GRACELAND IN MEMPHIS, TENNESSEE

The Life of Elvis Presley

In keeping with the traditions of the American Dream, it is no surprise that Elvis Aaron Presley was born into poverty on January 8, 1935, in East Tupelo, Mississippi.

Remembering those hard times, Elvis made a promise to his mother that, when he grew up, they would never be poor again. What followed was a series of events that undoubtedly helped him to keep that promise. The first was his exposure to music at a young age while attending church. The second was a $12.95 guitar he received as a gift. And the third was when he moved with his mother and father to Memphis, Tennessee.

While attending L.C. Humes High School, Elvis made plenty of friends. His polite, shy, country ways also earned him the respect of his teachers. It was this charm that would continue into his days as one of the world's most influential entertainers.

Elvis helped to support his family by working a variety of odd jobs, including as a truck driver and movie usher. With his busy schedule, he still found the time to sing in the school's annual Christmas concert.

In July of 1953, he walked into the Memphis Recording Studio and recorded the singles "My Happiness" and "That's When Your Heartache Begins." The recordings were to be a birthday gift for his mother, Gladys. The owner of the studio, Sam Phillips, had Elvis come back to record two more songs, "Casual Love Affair" and "I'll Never Stand in Your Way." It was now apparent that the many hours Elvis had spent in front of the radio, mimicking the songs he heard, was about to pay off. As one critic would later say, "Elvis has set the music world afire."

In the summer of 1954, Elvis linked up with guitarist Scotty Moore and bass player Bill Black, forming a group called The Blue Moon Boys.

They performed at county fairs and local clubs. For the first time, Elvis was making money from his unique style of music.

Eventually Elvis met up with Colonel Tom Parker, who became his life-long manager. It was the Colonel who exposed Elvis's unique talents to the world. In November 1955, the Colonel negotiated a deal with RCA to buy Elvis's contract from Sun Records. In January of 1956, "Heartbreak Hotel" hit the airwaves, followed by "Blue Suede Shoes."

The more public Elvis became, the more his fans screamed for him. There were also the loud outcries warning of Elvis's "bad influence" on the nation's youth by civic leaders and various church groups. But Elvis's fans increased with such rapidly growing numbers that in 1956 *Variety* magazine crowned him the "King of Rock and Roll."

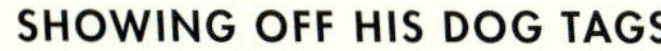

SHOWING OFF HIS DOG TAGS

TAKING TIME OUT FROM TRAINING TO READ A FAN MAGAZINE

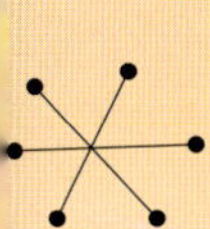

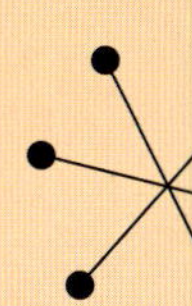

The next step for Elvis was television. From the first time he appeared in living rooms across the nation, his popularity soared. From there Hollywood beckoned, and Elvis jumped to the big screen. Elvis's first film, *Love Me Tender*, released by 20th Century Fox, earned him a million dollars. The critics panned Elvis's acting ability, but his fans loved him. Fan clubs sprouted up all over the globe, and Elvis received as many as five thousand letters a day.

In late 1957, with his career in full swing, Elvis received his draft notice from the US Army. To make sure he would not be forgotten while stationed in Germany, the Colonel had Elvis record music that was to be released during his absence. While he was training in Texas, word came that his mother had passed away. Her death was a blow to Elvis. And while he was stationed in Germany, Elvis met Priscilla Beaulieu, the daughter of a US Air Force officer.

Upon Elvis's return to the United States, the Colonel lined up a guest appearance for him on Frank Sinatra's television special. It was the Colonel's way of letting the fans know that Elvis was back in action. This was followed by the release of another film, *G.I. Blues*.

Gossip columnists were now linking Elvis romantically with his leading ladies, but it was Priscilla who had captured Elvis's heart. In 1960 she spent Christmas with him at Graceland. During their long courtship, Elvis continued to record songs that turned into gold records as well as make movies in Hollywood. With more than enough money rolling in, Elvis donated a considerable amount to various charities. For himself he bought expensive cars and jewelry.

On May 1, 1967, Elvis and Priscilla were married in a private ceremony held in Las Vegas. Nine months later, Elvis became a father. Of his daughter, Lisa Marie, Elvis said, "One of the greatest moments of my life comes when she looks up and smiles just for me."

As Priscilla and Lisa Marie settled into life at Graceland, Elvis continued to perform in concert, record music, and make movies. Priscilla, who grew tired of the somewhat lonely lifestyle, separated from Elvis in 1972. A year later their divorce was final.

With the failure of his marriage, Elvis poured himself into his work. Plagued by ill health, he would not slow down for fear of disappointing his fans. In August of 1977, Elvis returned to Graceland to rest before his next series of concert appearances. On August 16, he died at the age of forty-two. The news of his death shocked the world. Millions mourned the country boy who became the King. Although his death has created an absence in the entertainment industry, millions continue to enjoy his music and films. And for his fans, Elvis left a legacy to be cherished.

Elvis loved Western films. He often rented a Memphis theater after hours so he and his friends could watch Westerns all night. At dawn they would stop at a nearby restaurant for breakfast or go to Graceland, where Gladys, his mother, would prepare griddle cakes and hominy grits for all of them.

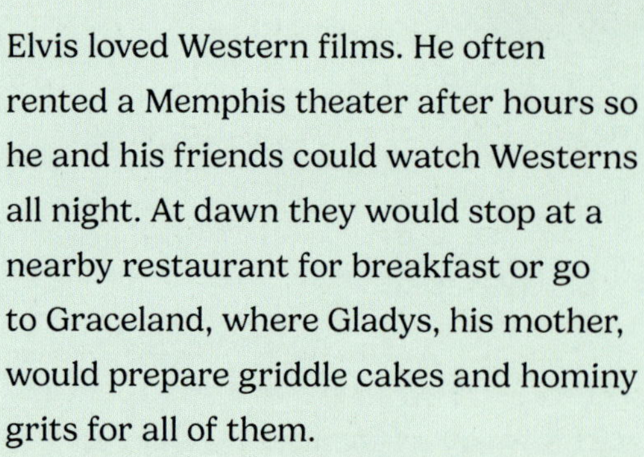

Elvis's Pantry

The following is a list of items that were kept on
hand in the kitchen for Elvis at all times.

One case regular Pepsi
One case orange drinks
Milk, including half-and-half (at least three bottles)
Fresh, hand-squeezed orange juice
Dinner rolls (he preferred premade Brown 'N Serve brand)
Cans of biscuits (at least six)
Hamburger buns
Fresh, lean ground meat
Thin, lean bacon
Ingredients for meat loaf and sauce
Wieners
Potatoes and onions
Pickles
Cans of sauerkraut
Mustard
Peanut butter
Assorted fresh fruit
Shredded coconut
Banana pudding (to be made each night)
Brownies
Fudge cookies
Ice cream (vanilla and chocolate)
**Chewing gum (three packs each of Wrigley's Spearmint,
Doublemint, and Juicy Fruit)**

Menus

The menus suggested here are just that: suggestions. You may want to vary them, exercising your own imagination. The combination for any menu is endless; these are only a guide to help you get started. All of these menus were created from dishes that Elvis especially enjoyed.

LET'S HAVE A PARTY
Garlic Dip
Stuffed Celery
Deviled Eggs
Fried Cheese Balls
Sweet-and-Sour Meatballs
Tomato Juice Cocktail

EARLY RISER BREAKFAST
Coffee and Tea
Orange Juice
Hominy Grits
Pan-Fried Potatoes
Blueberry Muffins
Griddle Cakes
Spanish Omelet

MORNINGS IN MEMPHIS
Coffee and Tea
Orange Juice
Hash Brown Potatoes
Baking Powder Biscuits
Melon Salad
French Toast
Scrambled Eggs

TRYING TO LOOK LIKE HIS IDOL JAMES DEAN

SUNDAY BRUNCH
Coffee and Tea
Tomato Juice Cocktail
Green Pea Salad
Fruit Salad
Cranberry Roast Pork
Crispy Fried Chicken
Buttermilk Biscuits
Apple Pie

THE GLADYS SPECIAL
Vegetable Soup
Potato Salad
Bacon and Tomato Sandwich
Fudge Cookies
Lemonade

NEVER-FAIL FAVORITE LUNCH
Milk
Peanut Butter and Banana Sandwich
Lemon Meringue Pie

HIGH NOON
Vegetable Soup
Cheeseburger
Pound Cake
Banana Pudding
Chocolate Malted Shake

WITH VERNON AND GLADYS BEFORE
LEAVING FOR KILLEEN, TEXAS

LUNCH COUNTER SPECIAL
Chicken Salad
Pear Salad
Strawberry Ice Cream
Cherry Pie
Milk

ENJOYING A DAY OF SUNSHINE

Two weeks before Elvis was to leave for the army, his mother invited his friends over to Graceland for a farewell party. Making sure there was plenty for everybody to eat, she prepared Elvis's favorite pork chops with mashed potatoes and gravy. For dessert everyone enjoyed her homemade apple pie.

COMPANY'S COMING

Coffee and Tea
Baking Powder Biscuits
Symphony of Green Salad
Fried Okra
Mashed Potatoes and Gravy
Pork Chops with Sauerkraut
Apple Pie

SUNDAY SUPPER

Coffee and Tea
Corn Bread
Vegetable Soup
Mustard Greens and Potatoes
Fried Okra
Meat Loaf
Coconut Cake

A SOUTHERN FEAST

Coffee and Tea
Coleslaw
Potato Salad
Crispy Fried Chicken
Corn Bread
Peach Cobbler
Southern Pecan Pie

A PICNIC IN THE PARK

Coleslaw
Potato Salad
Deviled Eggs
Baked Beans
Cheeseburgers
Lemonade

FAMILY BARBECUE

Coleslaw
Hush Puppies
Ham Salad
Fried Okra
Maple Spareribs
Strawberry Ice Cream
Pineapple Soda

ENJOYING A GAME OF TOUCH FOOTBALL

GARDEN PARTY

Stuffed Celery
Deviled Eggs
Corn Bread
Green Pea Salad
Cornish Game Hens
Peanut Butter Pie

LAS VEGAS SPECIAL

Vegetable Soup
Baking Powder Biscuits
Baked Beans
Crispy Fried Chicken
Chocolate Malted Shake
Blueberry Pie

A JANUARY BIRTHDAY BASH

Cheeseburgers
Pork Chops with Sauerkraut
Mashed Potatoes and Gravy
Peanut Butter and Banana Sandwich
Coconut Cake
Chocolate Malted Shake

CHRISTMAS IN MEMPHIS

Coffee and Tea
Baking Powder Biscuits
Vegetable Soup
Green Pea Salad
Cranberry Squash
Turkey with Stuffing and Gravy
Apple Pie

At Christmas, Elvis was always home with his family at Graceland. There would be plenty of packages under a huge tree. He served the traditional turkey with stuffing, but for himself Elvis preferred ham salad, potato salad, meat loaf, and monkey bread.

Appetizers

GARLIC DIP

PEPPER-STUFFED MUSHROOMS

CHICKEN LIVERS WRAPPED IN BACON

STUFFED CELERY

FRIED CHEESE BALLS

HUSH PUPPIES

CELERY-CHEESE BALLS

SWEET-AND-SOUR MEATBALLS

BARBECUE SAUCE I

BARBECUE SAUCE II

DEVILED EGGS

DILL DIP

Garlic Dip

MAKES ABOUT 2 CUPS

1 clove garlic, minced
3 tablespoons garlic juice
4 ounces cream cheese, softened

1 cup sour cream
Raw vegetables or assorted
crackers

1. In a small mixing bowl, stir the minced garlic with the garlic juice. Add the cream cheese and sour cream, stirring until thoroughly combined.

2. Spoon the dip into a serving dish. Refrigerate before serving. Serve with raw vegetables or assorted crackers.

Elvis Presley was born around noon on January 8, 1935, in the farm community of East Tupelo, Mississippi. In this town of eleven thousand, there was a movie theater, a department store, cotton mills, a Carnation Milk plant, and textile plants.

His mother, Gladys, worked as a seamstress, and his father, Vernon, was a carpenter. They lived as sharecroppers in a two-room shotgun house, and they attended the First Assembly of God Church. For entertainment they would sing on their front porch or hang out at the local grocery store.

ELVIS WITH HIS MOTHER AND FATHER,
GLADYS AND VERNON PRESLEY

Pepper-Stuffed Mushrooms

MAKES 1 DOZEN

12 large mushrooms
2 tablespoons olive oil
2 small cloves garlic, minced

2 jalapeño peppers, chopped
2/3 cup grated Monterey Jack
cheese, divided

1. Using your hands, tear the mushroom stems away from the mushroom caps. Set the caps aside, then finely chop the stems.
2. In a 12-inch skillet over medium-low heat, heat the oil and sauté the mushroom caps for about 10 minutes. Once soft, remove the caps from the skillet, and place them on a paper towel–lined plate to drain.
3. Using the oil remaining in the skillet, sauté the chopped mushroom stems, garlic, and jalapeño peppers for about 10 minutes. Preheat the oven on the Broil setting. Transfer the mushroom stem mixture to a large mixing bowl. Add 1/2 cup of the Monterey Jack cheese, and stir until the cheese is evenly dispersed.
4. Fill the mushroom caps with the stem mixture, and top with the remaining cheese. Broil the stuffed mushrooms until the cheese melts and bubbles. Serve hot.

Chicken Livers Wrapped in Bacon

MAKES 4 SERVINGS

3/4 pound chicken livers
1/2 teaspoon salt
Black pepper to taste
5 drops onion juice

6 slices bacon
1 tablespoon finely chopped fresh parsley

1. Preheat the oven on the Broil setting. Clean the chicken livers thoroughly in cold water. Pat dry with paper towels. Lay the livers on wax paper. Sprinkle with salt, black pepper, and onion juice. Set aside.

2. Cut the bacon slices in half crosswise. Wrap each piece around a chicken liver. Fasten the bacon to the livers with a 4-inch skewer, and place the skewers on a sheet pan lined with aluminum foil.

3. Broil the skewers for about 7 minutes or until the bacon is thoroughly browned. Turn the skewers, and brown the other side until the chicken livers reach an internal temperature of 165°F and the bacon is evenly browned.

4. Briefly place the skewers on a paper towel–lined plate to drain excess grease, then move them to a serving platter. Pour remaining pan juices over the skewers, sprinkle with parsley, and serve.

Elvis's earliest recollection of music was with his parents at the First Assembly of God Church. At the age of three he would run over to join the choir, singing the hymns. Although he didn't always know the words, he could carry a tune. After supper Gladys would teach him the words to the hymns, and along with Vernon they would harmonize together.

Stuffed Celery

MAKES 1 DOZEN

Cream Cheese Filling

1¹/2 ounces cream cheese, softened
2 tablespoons mayonnaise
4 pimiento-stuffed olives, chopped

2 tablespoons finely chopped
  pecans
Salt to taste

Blended Cheese Filling

3 ounces cream cheese, softened
1 tablespoon Roquefort cheese

1 tablespoon butter
Salt to taste

Egg Filling

1 hard-boiled egg, finely chopped

2 tablespoons mayonnaise

Stuffed Celery

3 ribs crisp celery

Prepared fillings

For the fillings

1. To make the Cream Cheese Filling, combine the cream cheese, mayonnaise, olives, pecans, and salt in a small bowl. Stir together until thoroughly mixed.
2. To make the Blended Cheese Filling, in a separate small bowl, combine the cream cheese, Roquefort cheese, butter, and salt. Stir together until thoroughly mixed.
3. To make the Egg Filling, in another small bowl combine the hard-boiled egg and mayonnaise. Stir together until thoroughly mixed.

To Assemble the Stuffed Celery

1. Cut each rib of celery into 4 pieces.
2. Spoon the Cream Cheese Filling onto 4 of the celery pieces. Spoon the Blended Cheese Filling onto 4 celery pieces. Spoon the Egg Filling onto the remaining celery pieces.
3. Refrigerate before serving.

Fried Cheese Balls

MAKES 2 DOZEN

Vegetable oil or another neutral oil,
  for frying
3 egg whites
1 tablespoon all-purpose flour

Salt to taste
1³/4 cups grated Cheddar cheese
1/2 cup breadcrumbs

1. In a large saucepan or Dutch oven over medium heat, heat 2 inches of oil to 375°F.
2. In a large mixing bowl, beat the egg whites until stiff. Set aside. In a medium mixing bowl combine the flour and salt. Slowly fold the flour mixture and the cheese into the egg whites until well combined.
3. Using a teaspoon, drop the dough into the breadcrumbs, coating well. Shape the dough into balls. Lower the balls into the hot oil, and fry for about 2 to 3 minutes or until golden brown. Remove the cheese balls, and place them on a paper towel–lined plate to drain. Serve warm or cold.

Hush Puppies

MAKES 2 DOZEN

Vegetable oil or another neutral oil,
  for frying
1/2 cup sifted all-purpose flour
1 cup cornmeal
1 medium onion, chopped

1¹/2 teaspoons baking powder
1 egg
1 teaspoon salt
1 teaspoon sugar
Milk

1. In a large saucepan or Dutch oven over medium heat, heat 2 inches of oil to 350°F.
2. In a large mixing bowl, combine the flour, cornmeal, onion, baking powder, egg, salt, and sugar. Stir together until thoroughly mixed, moistening with just enough milk to create a stiff dough.
3. Scoop a rounded teaspoon of batter, and drop the batter into the hot oil. Repeat until the pan is full but not overcrowded. Fry the hush puppies for about 3 minutes, or until golden brown. Remove the hush puppies. Serve warm.

Fried Cheese Balls

Celery-Cheese Balls

MAKES 1 DOZEN

1 cup finely chopped celery
3 ounces cream cheese, softened
Salt and black pepper to taste

1 tablespoon chopped fresh
  parsley
Paprika

1. In a medium mixing bowl, blend the celery with the cream cheese. Season with salt and black pepper.
2. Shape the celery mixture into 12 balls and roll in the parsley. Sprinkle with paprika.
3. Arrange the balls on a serving plate, and refrigerate until firm.

ELVIS'S FIRST STARRING FILM ROLE WAS IN
LOVE ME TENDER WITH DEBRA PAGET.

Sweet-and-Sour Meatballs

MAKES 4 DOZEN

Meatballs

1/3 cup breadcrumbs

1/2 cup half-and-half

3 tablespoons butter, softened, divided

2 tablespoons finely chopped onion

3/4 pound ground beef

1/4 pound ground pork

3/4 teaspoon salt

3/4 teaspoon sugar

1/4 teaspoon black pepper

Sweet-and-Sour Sauce

2 tablespoons cornstarch

1/2 teaspoon salt

1/4 cup firmly packed light brown sugar

1/4 cup vinegar

1 cup pineapple juice

1 tablespoon soy sauce

For the meatballs

1. In a large mixing bowl, combine the breadcrumbs, half-and-half, and 1/2 cup water. Set the mixture aside.

2. In a large, heavy-bottomed skillet, melt 1 tablespoon of the butter and sauté the onion until transparent. Transfer the onion to a separate mixing bowl, and set the skillet aside. Add the ground beef, ground pork, salt, sugar, black pepper, and breadcrumb mixture. Mix well until thoroughly combined. Shape the meat into balls about 3/4 inch in diameter.

3. In the same skillet over medium heat, melt the remaining 2 tablespoons butter. Add the meatballs to the skillet and brown, turning frequently to cook evenly. Reduce the heat to low and cover the skillet. Continue to cook the meatballs for about 10 minutes, turning frequently.

For the sauce

1. While the meatballs cook, in a small saucepan stir the cornstarch, salt, brown sugar, vinegar, pineapple juice, and soy sauce until combined. Cook over medium heat until thick, stirring constantly.

2. When the meatballs are done cooking or register an internal temperature of 160°F, pour the sauce over the meatballs and serve.

Barbecue Sauce II

Barbecue Sauce I

MAKES ABOUT 2 CUPS

1 cup dry red wine
1 (6-ounce) can tomato paste
1/4 cup olive oil
1 1/2 teaspoons crushed oregano

2 cloves garlic, minced
1/4 teaspoon salt
1/2 teaspoon black pepper

1. In a small mixing bowl, stir together the red wine, tomato paste, olive oil, oregano, garlic, salt, and black pepper.
2. Serve alongside your meal, and refrigerate any unused portion.

Barbecue Sauce II

MAKES ABOUT 12 CUPS

3 1/2 cups ketchup
1 1/2 cups chili sauce
1/3 cup yellow mustard
1 teaspoon dry mustard
1 1/2 cups firmly packed light brown
    sugar
1 1/2 cups red wine vinegar

1 cup fresh lemon juice
1/2 cup thick steak sauce
Hot pepper sauce to taste
1/4 cup Worcestershire sauce
1 tablespoon soy sauce
1 tablespoon oil
1 1/2 cups beer

1. In a large mixing bowl, stir together the ketchup, chili sauce, yellow mustard, dry mustard, brown sugar, red wine vinegar, lemon juice, steak sauce, hot pepper sauce, Worcestershire sauce, soy sauce, oil, and beer.
2. Serve alongside your meal, and refrigerate any unused portion.

Deviled Eggs

MAKES 1 DOZEN

2 slices bacon
6 hard-boiled eggs, peeled
1/2 teaspoon salt
1/8 teaspoon black pepper

1/4 teaspoon dry mustard
1 1/2 teaspoons apple cider vinegar
Paprika to taste
Chopped chives for garnish (optional)

1. In a 12-inch skillet over medium-high heat, fry the bacon until crisp. Transfer the bacon to a paper towel–lined plate and allow it to cool. Crumble the bacon into small pieces. Set aside.
2. Slice the hard-boiled eggs in half lengthwise. Remove the yolks, taking care not to tear the egg whites, and add the yolks to a medium mixing bowl. Place the egg whites on a serving dish, and set aside. In the mixing bowl mash the egg yolks with the bacon, salt, black pepper, dry mustard, and apple cider vinegar. Mix until smooth.
3. Using a spoon or piping bag, fill the centers of the egg whites with the egg yolk mixture. Sprinkle with paprika and chopped chives, if using, and serve.

Dill Dip

MAKES 2 CUPS

2 cups sour cream
2 cups mayonnaise
1 tablespoon chopped fresh parsley

1 tablespoon dried onion flakes
1 teaspoon dried dill weed
Raw vegetables or assorted crackers

1. In a small mixing bowl, mix the sour cream with the mayonnaise. In a separate small bowl, combine the parsley, dried onion flakes, and dill weed. Add the spice mixture to the sour cream mixture, and stir until combined.
2. Spoon the dip into a serving dish. Refrigerate overnight. Serve with raw vegetables or assorted crackers.

Deviled Eggs

Soups and Salads

TOMATO SOUP

VEGETABLE SOUP

JAMBALAYA

SPLIT PEA SOUP

POTATO SALAD

CHICKEN SALAD

COLESLAW

HAM SALAD

MELON SALAD

GREEN PEA SALAD

BAKED BANANAS

FRUIT SALAD

PEAR SALAD

SYMPHONY OF GREEN SALAD

Tomato Soup

Tomato Soup

3 tablespoons butter, divided
2 tablespoons all-purpose flour
2 cups beef stock
1 carrot, chopped
2 ribs celery, chopped
1 small turnip, chopped

2 leeks, chopped
1/4 cup lean cooked ham
2 cups diced canned tomatoes
Salt and black pepper to taste
1 tablespoon finely chopped chives

1. In a large saucepan over medium heat, melt 2 tablespoons of the butter. Stir in the flour and cook, stirring constantly, for about one minute. Add the beef stock, carrot, celery, turnip, leeks, and ham and simmer for about 30 minutes.
2. Add the tomatoes, and season with salt and black pepper to taste. Slowly bring the soup to a bowl over medium-high heat, then reduce heat and summer for another 20 minutes.
3. Strain the soup through a sieve. Add the remaining 1 tablespoon butter and the chives, stirring to incorporate, then serve.

Vegetable Soup

1 1/2 pounds bone-in beef shank
2 quarts cold water
1/2 cup chopped carrots
1/2 cup canned lima beans, drained and rinsed
1/3 cup chopped onion

1/3 cup chopped cabbage
1/3 cup diced celery
1/3 cup green peas, shelled
1 1/2 teaspoons salt
Black pepper to taste

1. Place the beef in a large stockpot or Dutch oven. Pour in the cold water to cover the beef. Place the pot on the stove and bring the water to a boil. Turn the heat to low, and simmer the beef for about 3 hours, or until the meat is tender and shreds easily with a fork. Remove the beef from the broth, and reserve it for another use.
2. Skim the fat off the top of the broth. Add the carrots, lima beans, onion, cabbage, celery, and peas, and simmer until tender. Season with salt and black pepper, then serve.

Jambalaya

MAKES 4–6 SERVINGS

2 tablespoons vegetable or
   canola oil
1 large onion, chopped
1 cup chopped green bell pepper
1 clove garlic, minced
1 cup diced cooked chicken
1 1/2 cups sliced smoked sausage
5 tomatoes, peeled and diced
3 cups chicken broth

1 cup uncooked white rice
1 tablespoon chopped fresh parsley
   (or 1 1/2 teaspoons dried parsley)
1/2 teaspoon fresh thyme
   (or 1/4 teaspoon dried thyme)
1/2 teaspoon salt
1 tablespoon hot pepper sauce
1 cup cooked shrimp

1. In a large stockpot or Dutch oven over medium heat, heat the oil. Sauté the onion, green bell pepper, and garlic until tender. Add the cooked chicken, smoked sausage, tomatoes, chicken broth, rice, parsley, thyme, salt, and hot pepper sauce. Stir until combined.
2. Bring the mixture to a boil, then reduce the heat to low and cover. Simmer for about 25 minutes, or until the rice is cooked and the liquid has been absorbed.
3. Add the cooked shrimp, and remove the pan from heat. Let the jambalaya stand for 5 minutes. Stir to evenly distribute the ingredients, then serve.

On October 3, 1945, Elvis made his first public appearance during Children's Day at the Mississippi-Alabama Fair and Dairy Show. For his part, Elvis stood on a chair and sang a song called "Old Shep." He won second place. In honor of the occasion, Gladys baked Elvis's favorite apple pie for dessert.

Split Pea Soup

MAKES 4–6 SERVINGS

1 pound dried split peas
3 quarts cold water
1 pound smoked ham hock or
   ham bone
2 bay leaves
1½ teaspoons salt

2 leeks, sliced
1 potato, peeled and cubed
1 pound smoked sausage, whole
Black pepper to taste
Hot pepper sauce to taste
Dried celery leaves (optional)

1. In a large stockpot or Dutch oven, cover the dried split peas with enough water to submerge them by two inches. Soak the peas overnight.

2. When you're ready to cook, drain the peas. Place the peas back in the stockpot or Dutch oven, and cover them with the cold water. Place the pot on the stove over medium-high heat, and bring to a boil.

3. Add the ham hock or ham bone, bay leaves, and salt. Cover the pot, turn the heat to low, and simmer about 1 hour 30 minutes, stirring occasionally. To the pot add the leeks and potato, stirring frequently. Simmer for about 15 minutes. Place the sausage in the pot. Simmer for about 20 minutes more.

4. Remove the sausage and ham hock from the soup. Cut any skin from the pork, and dice the meat into 1-inch cubes. Slice the sausage. Place the pork and sausage back in the soup pot.

5. Remove the bay leaves. Season the soup with black pepper, hot pepper sauce, and dried celery leaves, if using, then serve.

ELVIS AT THE FRONT DOOR OF GRACELAND

ENJOYING A BOWL OF SOUP IN GERMANY

Potato Salad

MAKES 8 SERVINGS

2 pounds small new potatoes
1 onion, chopped
2 hard-boiled eggs, chopped
1 cup diced celery

3/4 cup mayonnaise
1 tablespoon mustard
3 tablespoons sweet pickle juice
Salt and black pepper to taste

1. In a large stockpot or Dutch oven, place the potatoes and cover them with water by two inches. Salt the water as desired. Boil the potatoes in salted water until tender. Drain the potatoes, then cool them to room temperature.
2. Evenly chop the potatoes, and place them in a large mixing bowl. Add the onion, eggs, and celery.
3. In a small mixing bowl stir the mayonnaise, mustard, pickle juice, salt, and black pepper until thoroughly combined.
4. Pour the mayonnaise mixture into the potato mixture, then toss until the potatoes are coated in the mayonnaise mixture. Refrigerate about 3 hours, then serve.

Elvis would sit for hours in front of the radio, listening to the *Grand Ole Opry*. He learned the songs by imitating the notes on his guitar. When he knew the song, he would then add his own style to make it uniquely his own.

Chicken Salad

MAKES 6 SERVINGS

$1/2$ cup chicken fat	3 cups diced cooked chicken
$1/2$ cup distilled white vinegar	2 cups diced celery
$1/2$ teaspoon onion juice	$1/4$ cup capers
Salt and black pepper to taste	Mayonnaise to taste

1. In a medium mixing bowl, stir the chicken fat, vinegar, onion juice, salt, and black pepper until combined.
2. Add the chicken to the bowl, and mix until the chicken is coated with the vinegar mixture. Let the chicken marinate in the fridge for about 2 hours, then drain the chicken.
3. In another large mixing bowl, add the drained chicken, celery, capers, and desired amount of mayonnaise. Refrigerate until chilled, then serve.

Note: Chicken fat can be substituted with $1/2$ teaspoon chicken bouillon.

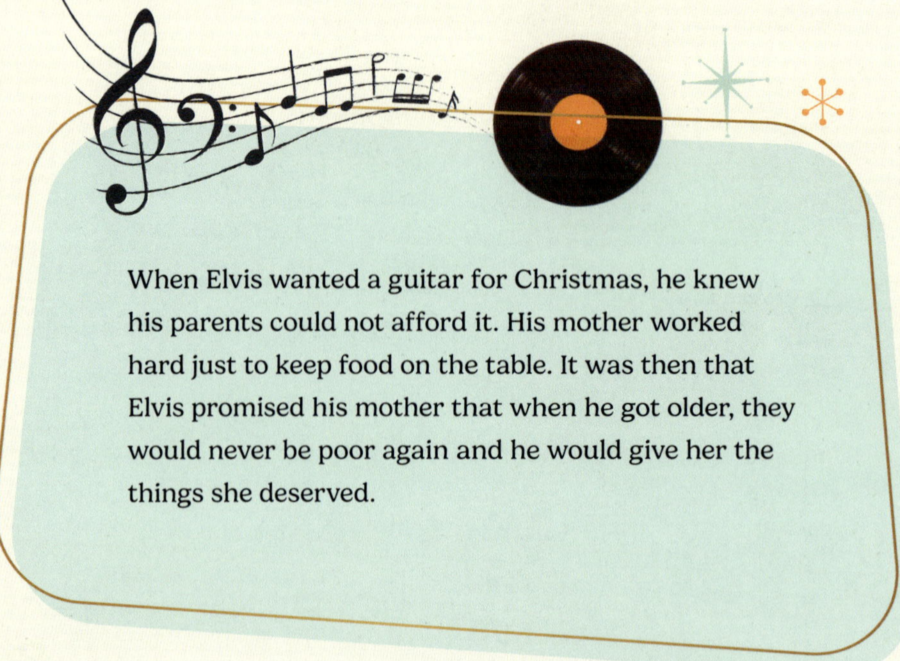

When Elvis wanted a guitar for Christmas, he knew his parents could not afford it. His mother worked hard just to keep food on the table. It was then that Elvis promised his mother that when he got older, they would never be poor again and he would give her the things she deserved.

WITH HIS FATHER, VERNON

Coleslaw

MAKES 8–10 SERVINGS

½ cup chopped onion
1 small head cabbage, chopped
2 teaspoons sugar

½ teaspoon vinegar
Mayonnaise to taste
Salt to taste

1. In a large mixing bowl, toss the onion and cabbage.
2. In a small mixing bowl, stir the sugar, vinegar, and 3 tablespoons water. Add to the cabbage mixture, and toss until combined. Stir in the desired amount of mayonnaise. Add the salt, and mix well.
3. Transfer the slaw to a large serving bowl. Refrigerate about 3 hours, then serve.

Ham Salad

MAKES 6 SERVINGS

2½ cups cubed cooked ham
1 cup diced celery
1 tablespoon fresh lemon juice
½ cup mayonnaise
1 tablespoon yellow mustard
1 tablespoon chopped sweet pickles

⅛ teaspoon black pepper
Salt to taste
Crumbled cooked bacon for garnish (optional)
Chopped green onions for garnish (optional)

1. In a large mixing bowl, combine the ham, celery, lemon juice, mayonnaise, mustard, pickles, black pepper, and salt. Toss thoroughly.
2. Transfer the salad to a large serving bowl. Refrigerate about 2 hours. Garnish with crumbled bacon and green onions, if desired, then serve.

ELVIS WITH ACTRESS
AND PHILANTHROPIST
YVONNE LIME

Melon Salad

Melon Salad

MAKES 12 SERVINGS

2 medium cantaloupes
2 medium honeydew melons
1 medium watermelon

1 pint fresh blueberries
Mint sprigs

1. Cut each of the cantaloupes, honeydew, and watermelon in half. Discard the seeds. Use a melon baller to scoop out the center of each melon half.
2. Place the melon balls in a large salad bowl. Pour in the blueberries and toss. Garnish the salad with mint sprigs, and serve.

Green Pea Salad

MAKES 4 SERVINGS

2 pounds fresh green peas, shelled
4 green onions

Mayonnaise to taste
Butter lettuce

1. Place the peas in a large saucepan, then cover them with enough water to submerge them by an inch. Salt the water as desired. Place the peas on the stove over medium-high heat, and heat until boiling. Cook until tender. Immediately drain the peas and place them under cold running water. Refrigerate the peas until chilled.
2. Meanwhile, thinly slice the green onions, including some of their green tops. When the peas are chilled, in a large mixing bowl combine the peas and green onions. Add mayonnaise to the pea mixture until the desired salad texture is reached.
3. Arrange the leaves of the butter lettuce to form cups. Spoon the salad into the lettuce cups, and serve.

Baked Bananas

MAKES 4 SERVINGS

4 bananas
Butter
Fresh lemon juice

Sugar
Chopped walnuts

1. Preheat the oven to 350°F. Butter an 8 x 8-inch baking pan and set aside.
2. Peel the bananas and cut them in half lengthwise. Place the bananas in the buttered baking dish and sprinkle with fresh lemon juice. Bake the bananas for 15 minutes.
3. Remove the bananas from the oven and sprinkle them with sugar. Return the bananas to the oven and bake for 5 more minutes.
4. Remove the bananas from the oven, top with walnuts, then serve.

Fruit Salad

MAKES 6 SERVINGS

1 medium honeydew melon
1 cup halved, pitted cherries
1 cup halved strawberries

1 cup pineapple chunks
2 tablespoons lime juice

1. Cut the honeydew melon in half lengthwise, and scoop out the seeds. Use a melon baller to scoop out the melon flesh. Reserve each hollow melon half for serving.
2. In a large mixing bowl, toss the honeydew, cherries, and strawberries with the pineapple chunks. Pour equal amounts of fruit into the center of each scooped-out melon half. Sprinkle lime juice over the fruit.
3. Refrigerate until chilled before serving.

Baked Bananas

TEDDY BEARS BECAME POPULAR WITH ELVIS FANS.

Pear Salad

MAKES 6 SERVINGS

1 (3-ounce) package lime gelatin
1 cup hot water
1 cup pear juice
1 tablespoon distilled white vinegar

Salt to taste
Dried ground ginger to taste
2 pears, peeled, cored, and diced
Shredded lettuce

1. In a small, heatproof mixing bowl, dissolve the gelatin in the hot water. Stir in the pear juice, vinegar, salt, and ground ginger, then refrigerate.
2. When the gelatin mixture is somewhat thickened, fold in the diced pears. Transfer the pear salad to a 4-cup mold, and refrigerate until completely thickened.
3. Unmold onto a bed of shredded lettuce, then serve.

Symphony of Green Salad

MAKES 12 SERVINGS

1 (3-ounce) package lime gelatin
1 cup hot water
2 cups small-curd cottage cheese
1 (8-ounce) can crushed pineapple,
  drained

1/3 cup mayonnaise
2 tablespoons fresh lemon juice
1/3 cup peeled and diced cucumber
1/2 cup chopped walnuts

1. In a small, heatproof mixing bowl, dissolve the gelatin in the hot water. Pour the gelatin into a 6-cup mold. Refrigerate the gelatin until it thickens.
2. In the gelatin mold, mix in the cottage cheese, crushed pineapple, mayonnaise, and lemon juice. Add in the cucumber and walnuts, and stir until the ingredients are evenly distributed.
3. Refrigerate the salad for about 7 hours, until firm. Unmold onto a serving dish and serve.

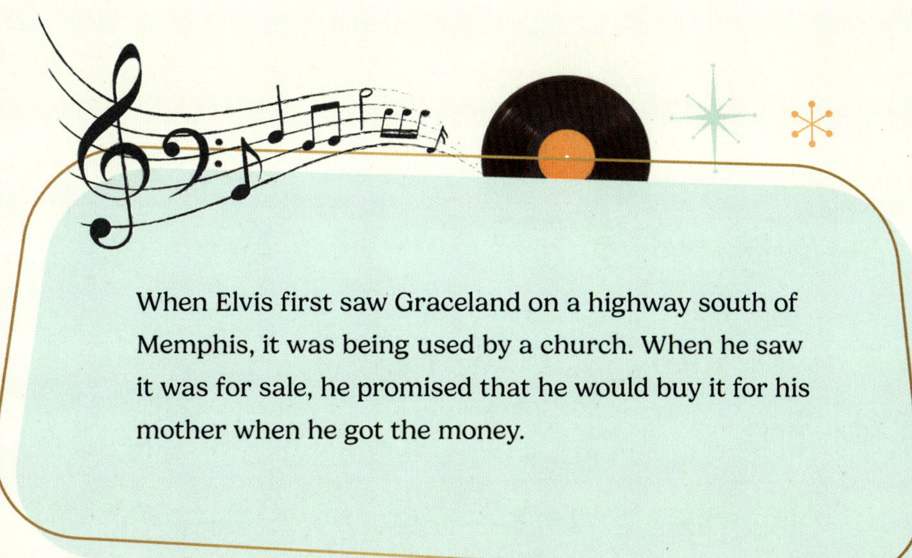

When Elvis first saw Graceland on a highway south of Memphis, it was being used by a church. When he saw it was for sale, he promised that he would buy it for his mother when he got the money.

Side Dishes

BAKED BEANS

CORN PUDDING

SCALLOPED OYSTERS

FRIED OKRA

HOMINY GRITS

SPINACH AND ARTICHOKE CASSEROLE

GRILLED ZUCCHINI

CRANBERRY SQUASH

PAN-FRIED POTATOES AND GRAVY

HASH BROWN POTATOES

CAROLINA SWEET POTATOES

MUSTARD GREENS AND POTATOES

MASHED POTATOES AND GRAVY

Baked Beans

MAKES 10 SERVINGS

2 pounds dried navy beans
2 quarts cold water
1 medium onion, sliced
1½ teaspoons salt
¼ cup apple cider vinegar
1 teaspoon yellow mustard

2 tablespoons firmly packed light brown sugar
½ cup molasses
¼ cup ketchup
Black pepper to taste
½ pound salt pork, sliced

1. Rinse the beans thoroughly, removing any stones or shriveled beans.
2. Place the beans in a large stockpot or Dutch oven, and cover them with the cold water. Bring the water to a boil over medium-high heat. Then cover, turn the heat to low, and simmer for about 30 minutes. Drain the beans, making sure to reserve their cooking liquid.
3. Preheat the oven to 250°F. Grease a 9 x 13-inch casserole dish. In the casserole dish, place the onion slices.
4. In a small mixing bowl, stir together the salt, apple cider vinegar, yellow mustard, brown sugar, molasses, ketchup, and black pepper.
5. Pour the mixture over the onions. Stir in the beans and 2½ cups of the reserved cooking liquid. Arrange the salt pork slices on top of the beans. Cover tightly with aluminum foil and bake for 4 hours.
6. After 4 hours remove 2 cups of beans and mash them thoroughly. Mix the mashed beans into the remaining beans. Cover the dish and bake for 3 to 4 more hours, or until the beans are tender. Add water as needed; the beans should be covered with a thick liquid. If you desire a thicker bean mixture, remove the cover about 1 hour before the beans are done.

WITH STELLA STEVENS IN *GIRLS! GIRLS! GIRLS!*

Corn Pudding

Corn Pudding

MAKES 6 SERVINGS

3 eggs
1 cup milk
1 tablespoon sugar
1 teaspoon salt
2 cups cream-style corn

2 tablespoons all-purpose flour
1 tablespoon minced onion
1/4 cup minced green bell pepper
1 tablespoon butter

1. Preheat the oven to 350°F. Grease a 2-quart casserole dish, and set aside.
2. In a large mixing bowl, lightly beat the eggs. Pour in the milk, sugar, and salt, and stir until combined. Add the corn, flour, onion, bell pepper, and butter, and mix until thoroughly combined.
3. Transfer the corn batter to the casserole dish. Bake uncovered for about 1 hour, until hot and bubbly.

Scalloped Oysters

MAKES 4 SERVINGS

2 cups oysters
4 tablespoons oyster juice
2 tablespoons half-and-half
1/2 cup stale breadcrumbs

1 cup crushed crackers
1/2 cup butter, melted
Salt and black pepper to taste

1. Preheat the oven to 450°F. Grease a 2-quart casserole dish.
2. In the casserole dish mix together the oysters, oyster juice, half-and-half, breadcrumbs, crackers, butter, salt, and black pepper until thoroughly combined.
3. Bake for about 30 minutes, until the oysters are hot and bubbly.

Fried Okra

Fried Okra

MAKES 6 SERVINGS

1 pound fresh okra
Vegetable oil for frying
1/2 cup cornmeal

1/4 teaspoon salt
Black pepper to taste
Dash of cayenne pepper

1. Heat a large stockpot of salted water over medium-high heat.
2. While the water is coming to a boil, cut off the stems and the tips of the okra pods. Wash the okra thoroughly. Once the water is boiling, add the okra and cook for about 8 minutes. Drain the okra and let them dry thoroughly.
3. In a large deep-frying pan or Dutch oven, heat 2 inches of oil to 350°F.
4. In a small mixing bowl, stir the cornmeal with the salt, black pepper, and cayenne pepper. Roll the okra in the seasoned cornmeal. Fry the okra until golden brown.

Note: If you're short on time, you can sauté the okra instead of frying. Melt 2 tablespoons butter in a frying pan, add the battered okra, and cook until golden brown.

Hominy Grits

MAKES 4 SERVINGS

2 teaspoons salt

1 cup hominy grits

1. In the top of a double boiler, add the salt and 5 cups water. Bring to a boil over direct medium heat. Add the hominy grits and boil for 10 minutes, whisking occasionally.
2. While the grits are boiling, add 2 inches of water to the bottom of the double boiler and bring to a simmer.
3. Once the grits have boiled for 10 minutes, remove the pot of boiling grits from the burner and place over the simmering water of the double boiler. Allow to cook in the top of the double boiler for about 2 hours, or until creamy.

Spinach and Artichoke Casserole

MAKES 6 SERVINGS

1 (14-ounce) can non-marinated
   artichoke hearts
3 (10-ounce) packages frozen
   chopped spinach
1 (8-ounce) package cream cheese,
   softened

2 tablespoons mayonnaise
6 tablespoons milk
Black pepper to taste
Grated Parmesan cheese to taste

1. Preheat the oven to 375°F. Grease a 2-quart casserole dish.
2. Drain the artichoke hearts, cut them in half, and place them in the casserole dish. Cover the artichoke hearts with the chopped spinach, and set aside.
3. In a medium mixing bowl, combine the cream cheese, mayonnaise, and milk. Spread the mixture over the spinach layer. Sprinkle with black pepper and Parmesan cheese.
4. Bake for about 35 to 40 minutes, until the casserole is hot and bubbly.

When asked how he felt about his lifestyle change after being drafted into the army, Elvis said, "I certainly don't mind the hard work. I've done plenty of it before this. Everybody keeps asking me what I'll do in the army. I'm going into the service and will do the best I can. If they want me to sing, I'll sing. If they want me to march—anything they want me to do is all right, whatever it is. I won't ask for special favors.

"The oddity is to get up and start running before breakfast. Breakfast is the one meal I count on. But the army isn't so rough. My folks had it rough. We lived in a housing project, and we were used to a hard life."

Grilled Zucchini

1 pound zucchini, sliced 1/4-inch thick
1 tablespoon olive oil
1 tablespoon grated Parmesan cheese

2 cups shredded mozzarella cheese
Salt and black pepper to taste
1/2 teaspoon dried oregano

1. Preheat the oven on the Broil setting.
2. Brush the zucchini slices with the olive oil, and arrange the slices in a 2-quart casserole dish. Sprinkle with the Parmesan cheese, mozzarella cheese, salt, black pepper, and oregano.
3. Broil for about 5 minutes, or until the zucchini is tender and the cheese is bubbly.

Cranberry Squash

MAKES 6 SERVINGS

1 pound raw winter squash, peeled
and cut into 1-inch cubes
1/2 cup fresh cranberries
1 small apple, chopped into 1/2-inch
slices

2 tablespoons raisins
Zest and juice from 1 small orange
1 tablespoon honey
1 tablespoon butter, melted
Salt to taste

1. Preheat the oven to 400°F. Grease a 2-quart casserole dish.
2. In the baking dish arrange the squash in a single layer on the bottom. Scatter the cranberries, apple slices, and raisins over the top.
3. Add the orange zest and juice, honey, melted butter, and salt, then toss to coat.
4. Cover the dish with aluminum foil, and bake for about 30 minutes or until the squash is tender.

Grilled Zucchini

Pan-Fried Potatoes

Pan-Fried Potatoes and Gravy

MAKES 4 SERVINGS

5 tablespoons butter, divided
6 medium new potatoes, sliced
Salt and black pepper to taste

1 tablespoon all-purpose flour
1 cup milk

1. In a 12-inch skillet over medium heat, melt 4 tablespoons of the butter. Add the sliced potatoes, and season with salt and black pepper. Cook until the potatoes are golden, turning frequently. Remove the potatoes to a warmed platter.
2. In the same skillet, over medium heat, melt the remaining 1 tablespoon butter. Stir in the flour and cook for about one minute, stirring constantly. Add the milk and season with salt and black pepper. Stir the gravy until it's thickened to your desired texture.
3. Pour the gravy over the potatoes, and serve.

Hash Brown Potatoes

MAKES 4 SERVINGS

3 large potatoes
2 tablespoons grated onion
1 teaspoon salt

Black pepper to taste
1/3 cup butter

1. Preheat the oven to 425°F.
2. Pierce the potatoes all over with a fork. Place the potatoes on a baking sheet, and bake for 1 hour, skin on, until the potatoes are tender. Let the potatoes cool thoroughly.
3. Once cooled, peel and thinly slice the potatoes to make 4 cups. In a large mixing bowl toss the potatoes with the grated onion, and season with salt and black pepper.
4. In a 12-inch skillet over medium heat, melt the butter. Add the potatoes to the skillet, and brown them for about 10 minutes. Reduce the heat to low, and continue cooking the potatoes for about 8 minutes or until golden brown.

Carolina Sweet Potatoes

Sweet Potatoes

3 cups cooked and mashed sweet
potatoes
1 cup sugar
2 eggs

1/2 cup butter, melted
1 teaspoon vanilla extract
1/2 cup milk

Topping

1 cup firmly packed light brown sugar
1/2 cup self-rising flour

1 cup chopped pecans
5 1/2 teaspoons butter

1. Preheat the oven to 350°F. Grease an 8 x 8-inch baking pan, and set aside.
2. In a large mixing bowl, combine the sweet potatoes, sugar, eggs, melted butter, vanilla, and milk. Transfer the potato mixture to the greased baking pan.
3. In a separate bowl mix the brown sugar, self-rising flour, and pecans until well combined. Cut in the butter until the butter looks like large pebbles in the sugar mixture.
4. Sprinkle the sugar mixture over the potatoes. Bake for about 30 minutes, or until bubbly.

Mustard Greens and Potatoes

MAKES 6 SERVINGS

2 ounces salt pork, thinly sliced
6 cups cold water
4 cups chopped mustard greens, stalks
and leaves separated

12 baby potatoes, peeled
Salt and black pepper to taste

1. In a large stockpot or Dutch oven, place the pork. Add the cold water, cover the pot, and simmer for about 1 hour.
2. Add the stalks of the mustard greens to the pork, and cook for about 15 minutes.
3. Add the potatoes and the tops of the mustard greens to the pot. Cook for about 15 minutes more.
4. Season with salt and black pepper, then serve.

Carolina Sweet Potatoes

Mashed Potatoes and Gravy

MAKES 6 SERVINGS

Potatoes

6 medium potatoes, peeled and
thinly sliced

1/2 cup hot milk

2 tablespoons butter

Salt to taste

Gravy

3 tablespoons fat of your choosing

3 tablespoons all-purpose flour

1/2 cup chicken stock

1 1/2 cups milk

Salt and black pepper to taste

Fresh parsley leaves for garnish
(optional)

For the potatoes

1. Fill a large stockpot or Dutch oven with water, and salt the water generously. Place the pot over medium-high heat, and bring the salted water to a boil.
2. Add the potato slices and boil until the potatoes are tender when pierced with a fork. Drain and return the potatoes to the pot.
3. Mash the potatoes with a fork. Add the hot milk and the butter. Beat with an electric mixer until light and fluffy. Add salt if needed.
4. Cover the pot, place it back on the stove, and turn the heat to low to keep the potatoes warm.

For the gravy

1. In a small saucepan melt the fat and stir in the flour. When the flour is blended into the fat but not browned, add the chicken stock and milk.
2. Stir the gravy constantly over low heat until it's smooth and thick. Season with salt and black pepper.

To assemble the dish

1. Spoon the mashed potatoes into a heated serving dish. Top with the gravy, garnish with rosemary, if using, and serve.

Breads

POPOVERS

FRENCH TOAST

BANANA BREAD

CRANBERRY BREAD

BLUEBERRY MUFFINS

BACON MUFFINS

SOURDOUGH STARTER

GRIDDLE CAKES

BAKING POWDER BISCUITS

CORN BREAD

SOURDOUGH BISCUITS

BUTTERHORNS

MONKEY BREAD

Popovers

MAKES 8 POPOVERS

2 eggs, room temperature, lightly beaten

1 cup milk, room temperature

1 cup all-purpose flour

$1/2$ teaspoon salt

1. Preheat the oven to 425°F. Grease 8 custard cups, and place the cups in the oven to warm them before filling.
2. In a large mixing bowl, combine the eggs, milk, flour, and salt.
3. Remove the cups from the oven, and fill each $1/3$ full with batter. Bake the popovers for 35 minutes until golden and cooked through.

French Toast

MAKES 4 SERVINGS

1 egg

$1/2$ cup cold milk

Butter

4 slices bread

1. In a large mixing bowl, whip the egg with the milk.
2. In a 12-inch skillet melt enough butter to coat the bottom of the pan.
3. Dip the sliced bread into the batter. Fry the dipped bread on both sides until browned.

While he was in the army, Elvis's mail averaged 15,000 letters a week He also received packages of cakes, pies, and cookies, which he shared with his fellow GI's.

Popovers

Banana Bread

MAKES 1 LOAF

$^1/_3$ cup butter

$^1/_2$ cup sugar

2 eggs

$1^3/_4$ cups all-purpose flour

1 teaspoon baking powder

$^1/_4$ teaspoon salt

1 cup mashed ripe bananas

1. Preheat the oven to 350°F. Grease a 9 x 5-inch loaf pan, and set aside.
2. In a large mixing bowl, cream the butter with the sugar. Add the eggs and beat well.
3. In a separate small mixing bowl, combine the flour, baking powder, and salt. Stir the flour mixture into the sugar mixture until thoroughly blended together. Add the bananas and mix well.
4. Pour the batter into the greased loaf pan, and bake for about 40 minutes. Remove the bread from the pan to cool.

POSING FOR THE MARCH OF DIMES IN 1957

Cranberry Bread

MAKES 1 LOAF

2 cups all-purpose flour
1 cup sugar
1 1/2 teaspoons baking powder
1/2 teaspoon baking soda
1/4 teaspoon salt
1/4 cup shortening

1 tablespoon orange zest
3/4 cup fresh orange juice
1 egg, beaten
1/2 cup chopped walnuts
2 cups coarsely chopped fresh cranberries

1. Preheat the oven to 350°F. Grease a 9 x 5-inch loaf pan, and set aside.
2. In a large mixing bowl, sift together the flour, sugar, baking powder, baking soda, and salt. Cut the shortening into the flour mixture until the mixture resembles coarse crumbs. Set aside.
3. In a separate small mixing bowl, combine the orange zest, orange juice, and egg.
4. Pour the juice mixture into the flour mixture, stirring until the batter is just moist. Carefully fold in the chopped walnuts and cranberries.
5. Spoon the batter into the greased loaf pan, spreading the batter into the corners and sides higher than in the center. Bake for 1 hour. Let the bread cool before serving.

Unknown to anyone, Elvis donated as much as $100,000 to the Elvis Presley Youth Foundation. This charity was for the poor and underprivileged children of Memphis. It was common for Elvis to share what he had with others, never forgetting where he came from.

Blueberry Muffins

MAKES 1 DOZEN

2 cups all-purpose flour	2/3 cup sugar
3 teaspoons baking powder	1 egg
1/2 teaspoon salt	3/4 cup milk
1/3 cup butter	1 cup blueberries

1. Preheat the oven to 425°F. Grease or line a 12-cup muffin pan, and set aside.
2. In a large mixing bowl, sift the flour with the baking powder and salt.
3. In a separate medium mixing bowl, cream together the butter and sugar. Add the egg and milk, and beat until fluffy.
4. Slowly pour the flour mixture into the creamed butter mixture, and mix until combined. Add the blueberries, and mix again.
5. Spoon the batter into the greased muffin cups, filling each cup 3/4 full. Bake for 18 minutes or until brown.

Bacon Muffins

MAKES 1 DOZEN

2 cups all-purpose flour	2 slices crisp bacon, crumbled
3 teaspoons baking powder	1 egg
1/4 teaspoon salt	1 cup milk
3 tablespoons sugar	2 tablespoons bacon fat, melted

1. Preheat the oven to 425°F. Grease or line a 12-cup muffin pan, and set aside.
2. Into a large mixing bowl, sift the flour. Add the baking powder, salt, and sugar, then sift the flour mixture 3 times. Stir in the bacon and set aside.
3. In a separate small mixing bowl, beat the egg with the milk and melted bacon fat.
4. Slowly stir the milk mixture into the flour mixture, stirring just until the batter comes together; it should be somewhat blended but not too smooth.
5. Spoon the batter into the greased muffin cups, filling each cup 2/3 full. Bake for 20 minutes or until brown. Serve hot.

Blueberry Muffins

Sourdough Starter

MAKES 3 CUPS

1 envelope active dry yeast
2 cups warm milk (115°F)

2 cups all-purpose flour

1. In a 1½-quart glass jar, combine the yeast, milk, and flour. Cover the top with a cheesecloth.
2. Leave the batter in a warm room for about 48 hours, stirring 2 to 3 times. The batter should ferment, bubble, and acquire a slightly sour smell.

To use the Sourdough Starter

1. Stir the starter and measure the amount needed for the recipe.
2. Add equal parts of flour and milk to the remaining portion of starter until it bubbles, and store using the instructions below.

To store the Sourdough Starter

1. To keep the starter active, place it in a pressure-sealed container. Cover the top and refrigerate the jar.
2. Every two weeks, add equal amounts of flour and milk to feed the starter. Never add anything but flour and milk to the starter. Keep refrigerated.

Minnie Mae, a tall, lanky woman lacking the stereotypical softness of grandmothers, liked to reminisce about her famous grandson's childhood in rural Mississippi.

"My grandmother cooks all my favorite dishes," Elvis told reporters.

Griddle Cakes 

MAKES 4 SERVINGS

1 cup sourdough starter (page 67)
2 cups warm milk
2¼ cups all-purpose flour
2 eggs

2 tablespoons sugar
2 tablespoons corn oil
⅓ cup cold milk
1 teaspoon baking soda

1. In a large mixing bowl, whisk together the sourdough starter, warm milk, flour, eggs, sugar, corn oil, cold milk, and baking soda. Let the batter sit for about 10 minutes.
2. Heat a griddle over medium-high heat. Spoon 4 to 5 tablespoons of the batter onto the griddle. Flip the griddle cake when the surface bubbles, and cook until golden brown.

Baking Powder Biscuits

MAKES 1 DOZEN

2 cups sifted all-purpose flour
½ teaspoon salt
2 teaspoons baking powder

¼ cup shortening
¾ cup milk

1. Preheat the oven to 450°F.
2. In a large mixing bowl, add the flour, salt, and baking powder. Cut the shortening into the flour mixture until the mixture resembles coarse crumbs. Add milk until the mixture becomes a soft dough. Mix lightly.
3. Flour the counter or a large board generously and turn the dough onto it. Knead the dough for about 2 minutes.
4. Roll the dough out to ½-inch thickness. Cut the biscuits with a floured 2½-inch biscuit cutter. Place the biscuits on an ungreased baking sheet. Bake for 12–15 minutes, or until golden brown.

Griddle Cakes

Corn Bread

Corn Bread

MAKES 1 LOAF

2 cups white cornmeal
1 cup all-purpose flour
1 tablespoon sugar
4 teaspoons baking powder

1 teaspoon salt
1 egg
Milk

1. Preheat the oven to 425°F. Grease a 9 x 5-inch loaf pan, and set the pan in the oven to warm.
2. In a large mixing bowl, combine the cornmeal, flour, sugar, baking powder, and salt. Stir in the egg and enough milk to make a smooth batter.
3. Pour the batter into the warm loaf pan. Bake for about 25 minutes or until golden brown.

Sourdough Biscuits

MAKES 2 DOZEN

1 cup whole wheat flour
1 cup all-purpose flour
1 tablespoon sugar
1 teaspoon baking powder

1/2 teaspoon salt
1/2 cup butter
2 cups sourdough starter (page 67)

1. Preheat the oven to 450°F. Lightly oil a baking sheet, and set aside.
2. In a large mixing bowl, sift together the wheat flour, all-purpose flour, sugar, baking powder, and salt. With a pastry blender cut in the butter until the mixture resembles coarse crumbs. Add the sourdough starter to the dough, and mix until thoroughly blended.
3. Flour the counter or a large board generously and turn the dough onto it. Lightly knead the dough.
4. Cut the dough into circles 2¹/₂ inches in diameter and place on the oiled baking sheet. Let the biscuits rise in a warm place for about 30 minutes. Bake the biscuits for 20 to 25 minutes until light brown.

IN THE STUDIO RECORDING HIS 1956 HIT SINGLE "HOUND DOG"

Butterhorns

MAKES 48 BUTTERHORNS

2 envelopes active dry yeast
1/2 cup warm water (115°F)
1/2 cup butter, softened
2/3 cup sugar
3 eggs, beaten

11/2 cups warm milk (115°F)
8 cups all-purpose flour
11/2 teaspoons salt
1/4 cup butter, melted

1. In a small mixing bowl, combine the yeast and warm water. Set aside.
2. In a large mixing bowl, cream the butter with the sugar. Stir in the eggs, warm milk, and yeast mixture. Slowly mix in the flour and salt a little at a time, until a dough forms. Place the dough in a greased mixing bowl. Cover and refrigerate for about 3 hours.
3. Remove the dough from the refrigerator and let it stand for about 15 minutes. Flour the counter or a large board generously and turn the dough onto it. Knead the dough lightly.
4. Divide the dough into 6 equal portions. Roll each dough portion into a circle about 9 inches in diameter. Cut each dough circle into 8 wedges. Brush each wedge with the melted butter. Starting with the wider end of each wedge, roll up the dough toward the point to make a horn.
5. Place the horns on an ungreased baking sheet lined with parchment paper. Let them rise for about 1 hour. Meanwhile, preheat the oven to 350°F. Bake the horns for about 15 minutes, or until golden brown.

Monkey Bread

MAKES 10 SERVINGS

Bread

2 envelopes active dry yeast
$1/2$ cup sugar, divided
$1/4$ cup warm water (115°F)
1 cup milk, heated

$1/3$ cup plus 1 tablespoon butter, softened
$1/2$ teaspoon salt
2 eggs, lightly beaten
$5^1/2$ cups all-purpose flour, divided

Topping

$1^1/2$ cups sugar
$1/2$ cup chopped walnuts or pecans
2 teaspoons fresh grated ginger

1 teaspoon ground cinnamon
$1/2$ cup butter, melted

1. In a small bowl dissolve the yeast and 1 tablespoon of the sugar in the warm water. Let the mixture stand for 5 minutes.

2. In a large mixing bowl, combine the heated milk, remaining 7 tablespoons sugar, butter, salt, and eggs. Stir in the yeast mixture. Mix in 3 cups of the flour, beating until smooth. Add the remaining flour and beat until combined.

3. Turn the dough onto a floured board and knead until it comes together, then let the dough rest for 10 minutes. Knead the dough for 8 minutes more.

4. Place the dough in a greased bowl, and turn the dough greased-side up. Cover the bowl and let the dough rise in a warm place until doubled in bulk, about 30 minutes.

5. Preheat the oven to 350°F. Grease a 10 x 4-inch loaf pan, and set aside.

6. In a small bowl combine the $1^1/2$ cups sugar, chopped nuts, grated ginger, and ground cinnamon, then set aside.

7. Punch down the dough and divide it into 36 portions. Roll each portion into a ball. Roll each ball first in the melted butter, then in the chopped nuts mixture. Place the balls in the greased loaf pan.

8. Sprinkle any remaining topping over the dough. Cover and let the dough rise for 30 minutes. Place the dough in the oven and bake for 1 hour or until golden brown. Let the bread cool before serving.

Main Dishes

CHEESEBURGERS

PEANUT BUTTER AND BANANA SANDWICH

CRANBERRY ROAST PORK

BACON AND TOMATO SANDWICH

CORNISH GAME HENS

PORK CHOPS WITH SAUERKRAUT

CHICKEN À LA KING

COUNTRY BAKED HAM

SPAGHETTI AND MEATBALLS

CRISPY FRIED CHICKEN

CHICKEN LIVERS WITH MUSHROOMS

MAPLE SPARERIBS

SPANISH OMELET

TURKEY WITH STUFFING AND GRAVY

SCRAMBLED EGGS

MEAT LOAF

Cheeseburgers

MAKES 6 BURGERS

1½ pounds ground beef

¼ cup cold milk

1 teaspoon salt

Black pepper to taste

⅓ cup chili sauce

3 tablespoons pickle relish

2 teaspoons yellow mustard

⅓ cup butter

6 hamburger buns, buttered and toasted

6 slices American cheese

1. Preheat the oven on the Broil setting. In a large mixing bowl, combine the ground beef, milk, salt, and black pepper. Form into 6 patties.
2. In a small bowl stir together the chili sauce, relish, and mustard.
3. In a 12-inch skillet melt the butter. Pan-fry the patties for about 12 minutes, turning several times as they cook.
4. Place the cooked patties on toasted hamburger bun bottoms set on top of a sheet pan. Spread the relish mixture on each patty. Top with cheese.
5. Move the sheet pan under the broiler, and cook the patties until the cheese begins to melt. Top with the burger bun tops, and serve.

Peanut Butter and Banana Sandwich

MAKES 5 SANDWICHES

¼ cup creamy peanut butter

2 very ripe bananas

10 slices buttered bread

Butter

1. In a small bowl mix the peanut butter with the banana until creamy.
2. Spread the mixture over 5 slices of the bread. Top each slice with the remaining bread.
3. In a 12-inch skillet melt enough butter to coat the bottom of the pan. Place the sandwiches in the butter and grill them until the bread is lightly toasted. Flip to grill the other side.
4. Place the sandwiches on a paper towel–lined plate, then serve.

Cheeseburgers

Cranberry Roast Pork

MAKES 6 SERVINGS

¾ cup fresh orange juice
¼ teaspoon ground cinnamon
¼ teaspoon ground ginger
1 (16-ounce) can whole berry
    cranberry sauce

¼ cup chopped onion
1 (4-pound) boneless pork roast,
    tied with string
Salt and black pepper to taste

1. Preheat the oven to 325°F.
2. In a saucepan combine the orange juice, cinnamon, ginger, cranberries, and onion. Bring the mixture to a boil and, when slightly thickened, remove the sauce from the heat.
3. Divide the sauce into two bowls: one for basting the pork, and one for serving at the table. Set the serving sauce aside.
4. Rub the roast with salt and black pepper, and place it on the rack of a broiler pan.
5. Bake the roast for 2½ to 3 hours, or until a meat thermometer registers at least 145°F. Halfway through baking, begin basting the roast every 15 minutes with the cranberry sauce; discard the basting sauce when the pork is done cooking.
6. Slice the pork and serve it with the reserved bowl of cranberry sauce on the side.

A girl dating Elvis usually found herself driving around for hours with him in his car, then stopping at a nondescript hamburger stand for a sandwich and a Coke.

Bacon and Tomato Sandwich

MAKES 4 SANDWICHES

2 medium tomatoes, sliced
8 slices buttered bread

8 slices crisp bacon

1. Arrange the sliced tomatoes on top of 4 slices of buttered bread. Place 2 strips of bacon on each sandwich. Top with the remaining bread slices.
2. Cut the sandwiches diagonally.

Note: Mayonnaise may be substituted for butter, if desired.

Cornish Game Hens

MAKES 2 SERVINGS

2 game hens
1 lemon
Salt to taste

1 cup half-and-half, divided
1^1/2 cups butter
1^1/2 cups green grapes

1. Preheat the oven to 375°F. Move the oven rack to the lowest position.
2. Rub the game hens with the juice of half a lemon. Sprinkle salt on the inside and outside of each bird. Place the hens in a 9 x 13-inch casserole dish.
3. Mix 2 tablespoons lemon juice with 2 tablespoons of the half-and-half, and spoon some of the mixture into each cavity. Skewer the cavities shut.
4. Bake the hens for 30 minutes, then baste with half-and-half. Bake for 10 more minutes, and baste the hens with half-and-half again. Bake for 10 more minutes, then pour the remaining half-and-half over the hens. Bake for a final 10 minutes, or until the internal temperature reaches 165°F.
5. Remove the hens to a serving platter. Stir the pan juices, and pour into a sauce dish.
6. In a 12-inch skillet melt the butter and lightly sauté the grapes. Arrange the grapes around the hens and serve immediately.

Bacon and Tomato Sandwich

Pork Chops with Sauerkraut

MAKES 8 SERVINGS

2 tablespoons butter
8 pork chops
Salt and black pepper to taste
2 (16-ounce) cans sauerkraut

2 tablespoons Dijon mustard
1/2 cup applesauce
1 tablespoon cornstarch
2 tablespoons cold water

1. Preheat the oven to 350°F. Grease a 9 x 13-inch casserole dish and set aside.
2. In a large skillet melt the butter. Place the pork chops in the skillet, and sauté until lightly browned on both sides. Season with salt and black pepper.
3. Rinse the sauerkraut under cold running water and drain the excess liquid. Place the sauerkraut in the casserole dish. Stir in the Dijon mustard and applesauce. Arrange the pork chops over the sauerkraut mixture. Cover and bake for 50 minutes, or until the pork reaches an internal temperature of at least 145°F.
4. In a small bowl dissolve the cornstarch in the cold water. Remove the pork chops to a separate plate. Stir the cornstarch slurry into the sauerkraut mixture to thicken, and serve alongside the pork chops.

RECORDING AT THE HISTORIC RCA STUDIO B IN NASHVILLE

Chicken à la King

MAKES 4 SERVINGS

1 (10-ounce) package frozen peas
1/3 cup butter
1/2 pound mushrooms, sliced
1/4 cup all-purpose flour
1/2 teaspoon salt
Black pepper to taste

1 1/2 cups chicken broth
1 1/2 cups heavy cream
1 (2-ounce) can pimiento strips
2 cups chopped cooked chicken
Buttered toast

1. Cook the peas according to the package directions. Set aside.
2. In a large Dutch oven, melt the butter, and sauté the mushrooms until tender. Remove the mushrooms and set them aside.
3. Stir the flour, salt, and black pepper into the butter remaining in the pan, whisking together until smooth. Heat until the mixture bubbles and thickens, about 4 minutes. Slowly add the chicken broth, cream, and pimiento strips. Cook until thickened.
4. Add the chicken, peas, and mushrooms. Cook, stirring constantly, for 5 minutes or until the chicken is heated through. Pour the mixture over buttered toast.

Country Baked Ham

MAKES 4 SERVINGS

1 (1-inch thick) ham steak
Black pepper and fresh or dried thyme
    to taste
1 1/2 cups canned tomatoes

1 cup shredded American cheese
1/4 cup minced onion
Fresh parsley, chopped

1. Preheat the oven to 350°F. Grease a 2-quart casserole dish. Place the ham in the greased casserole dish. Season with black pepper and thyme.
2. In a medium mixing bowl, stir together the tomatoes, cheese, onion, and parsley. Pour the mixture over the ham.
3. Cover the casserole dish tightly with aluminum foil and bake for about 45 minutes, turning the ham about halfway through the baking process. Remove from the oven, allow to rest for 10 to 15 minutes, then serve.

Chicken à la King

Spaghetti and Meatballs

MAKES 4 SERVINGS

Sauce

3 tablespoons butter
½ cup chopped onion
1 clove garlic, minced
3½ cups canned tomatoes

1 (6-ounce) can tomato paste
1 teaspoon salt
Black pepper to taste
Dried oregano to taste

Meatballs

½ pound ground beef
½ pound ground pork
1 cup breadcrumbs
1 tablespoon finely chopped fresh parsley

1 egg, beaten
Salt and black pepper to taste
2 tablespoons all-purpose flour
3 tablespoons butter

To Assemble

1 pound spaghetti

¼ cup grated Parmesan cheese

For the sauce

1. In a large skillet over medium heat, melt the butter, and sauté the onion and garlic until transparent.
2. Remove the skillet from the heat and stir in the tomatoes, tomato paste, salt, black pepper, and dried oregano.
3. Place the skillet back over medium heat, until simmering. Lower the heat to low, and simmer for 1 hour.

For the meatballs

1. In a large mixing bowl, combine the ground beef and ground pork. Mix in the breadcrumbs, parsley, egg, salt, and black pepper until thoroughly combined.
2. Shape the meat mixture into 1-inch balls. On a large plate sprinkle the flour. Roll the meatballs in the flour.
3. In a large skillet over medium heat, melt the butter and brown the meatballs. Drain the fat from the skillet.
4. Pour the sauce over the meatballs. When the sauce begins to simmer, reduce the heat to low, cover the pan, and simmer for 20 minutes.

To assemble the dish

1. While the meatballs and sauce are simmering, prepare the spaghetti according to the package directions.
2. When the spaghetti is done cooking, toss the sauce and meatballs with the noodles. Place the spaghetti on a serving platter and top with Parmesan cheese.

Crispy Fried Chicken

MAKES 4 SERVINGS

Vegetable oil for frying
1 cup pancake mix
Salt to taste

1 (2-pound) fryer chicken, cut into 8 pieces

1. In a large Dutch oven, heat the oil to 350°F.
2. In a large mixing bowl, stir together the pancake mix, salt, and 3/4 cup water. Beat 3 minutes to thoroughly blend. Dip the chicken pieces in the batter, and drain off the excess batter.
3. Deep-fry the chicken in the hot oil for 10 minutes or until golden brown and the internal temperature reaches 165°F. Drain the chicken on a paper towel–lined plate, and serve.

Chicken Livers with Mushrooms

MAKES 4 SERVINGS

1/4 pound chicken livers
1 teaspoon salt
1/4 cup all-purpose flour, divided
1/4 cup butter
1 onion, chopped

1 1/2 cups sliced mushrooms
1 cup chicken broth
1 cup milk
Black pepper to taste
Toast

1. Wash the chicken livers in cold water. Drain and pat dry. Place the livers on top of waxed paper. Sprinkle with salt and 2 tablespoons of the flour to coat.
2. In a skillet melt the butter and sauté the onion for 3 minutes. Add the livers and cook until lightly browned on the bottom. Turn the livers and add the mushrooms, allowing the mushrooms to cook undisturbed for about 5 minutes, until browned. Push the livers and mushrooms to one side of the skillet.
3. Blend the remaining 2 tablespoons flour into the fat in the pan. Slowly pour in the broth, milk, and black pepper. Cook for 5 minutes, stirring to keep smooth.
4. When the sauce thickens, serve the mixture over toast.

Crispy Fried Chicken

Maple Spareribs

MAKES 4 SERVINGS

3 pounds lean pork spareribs,
    trimmed of all excess fat
1/2 cup yellow mustard
1 cup cold water
1/2 cup tomato puree
1/2 cup maple syrup, divided

1/4 cup apple cider vinegar
1/2 cup finely chopped onion
1/4 cup Worcestershire sauce
1/2 teaspoon hot pepper sauce
1 1/2 teaspoons salt
1/2 teaspoon ground black pepper

1. Preheat the oven on the Broil setting. Pat the spareribs with a paper towel until they are completely dry, then cut them in half. Brush them thoroughly with mustard. Lay the ribs fat side up on the rack of a broiler pan. Broil the spareribs 4 inches from the heat for 5 minutes. Turn the ribs meat side up and broil them about 5 minutes longer.

2. Remove the ribs from the pan. Discard all of the fat that accumulated at the bottom of the pan, and pour the cold water into the broiler pan. Return the ribs to the pan, and set aside.

3. In a medium mixing bowl, combine the tomato puree, 1/4 cup of the maple syrup, apple cider vinegar, onion, Worcestershire sauce, hot pepper sauce, salt, and black pepper. Mix well. Stir in the remaining 1/4 cup maple syrup. With a pastry brush, spread 1/4 cup of the sauce over the ribs.

4. Reduce the oven temperature to 350°F. Lower the oven rack and place the ribs in the middle of the oven. Bake the spareribs for 1 hour, or until the ribs are brown and crisp and reach an internal temperature of at least 145°F. Baste the ribs with the sauce every 15 minutes.

ELVIS BEING GREETED BY FANS IN GERMANY

Spanish Omelet

MAKES 1 SERVING

4 tablespoons butter, divided
1 small onion, chopped
1/2 cup diced green bell pepper
1/4 cup diced red bell pepper
1 (6-ounce) can tomato paste

3/4 teaspoon Worcestershire sauce
Salt and black pepper to taste
1/4 pound mushrooms, chopped
3 large eggs
3 tablespoons milk

1. In a medium skillet melt 2 tablespoons of the butter. Add the onion and sauté until tender. Add the green bell pepper, red bell pepper, and tomato paste. Cook until the peppers are tender. Add the Worcestershire sauce and season with salt and black pepper.
2. In a separate small skillet, melt 1 tablespoon of the butter and sauté the mushrooms for about five minutes. Then fold the sautéed mushrooms into the tomato mixture.
3. In a small bowl beat the eggs with the milk. In the skillet used for the mushrooms, melt the remaining 1 tablespoon butter. Pour the eggs into the skillet and cook over medium-low heat until partially set.
4. Pour some of the tomato mixture over half of the eggs. Fold over half of the omelet, enclosing the mixture. Let the top set.
5. Flip the omelet onto a plate and spoon the remaining tomato mixture over the top.

Turkey with Stuffing and Gravy

MAKES 8 TO 12 SERVINGS

Stuffing

8 cups soft bread cubes
1 1/2 teaspoons salt
1 teaspoon dried sage
3/4 cup milk

1/3 cup chopped celery
1/3 cup chopped onion
1/4 teaspoon black pepper
3/4 cup butter, melted

Turkey

1 (12-pound) ready-to-cook turkey
2 teaspoons salt

1 cup butter, melted

Gravy

2 cups chicken broth
1/4 cup all-purpose flour

1/4 teaspoon salt
Black pepper to taste

For the stuffing

1. In an extra-large mixing bowl, combine the bread cubes, salt, and sage.
2. Add in the milk, celery, onion, black pepper, and melted butter. Toss thoroughly.

For the turkey

1. Preheat the oven to 325°F.
2. Rinse and dry the turkey. Rub the cavity with salt.
3. On the rack of a roasting pan, place the turkey breast-side up. Spoon the stuffing into the cavity of the turkey and skewer the opening shut. Place any remaining stuffing in a greased baking dish.
4. Brush the turkey with the melted butter. Bake the turkey for 4 hours or until a meat thermometer registers 190°F when inserted into the turkey and 165°F when inserted into the stuffed cavity. Baste occasionally with the pan drippings during baking.
5. Let the turkey cool for 30 minutes. Meanwhile, bake any remaining stuffing at 350° for about 20 minutes, or until browned.

For the gravy
1. In a large saucepan over medium-high heat, bring the chicken broth to a boil.
2. In a blender mix the flour with $1/2$ cup water until smooth.
3. Slowly pour half of the flour mixture into the broth, and season with salt and black pepper. Return the mixture to a boil, adding the remaining flour mixture as needed for the desired thickness.
4. Serve the gravy with the turkey and stuffing.

Scrambled Eggs

4 eggs
2 tablespoons heavy cream or milk
Salt and black pepper as desired
2 slices cooked bacon, crumbled,
    plus more whole slices for serving
    (optional)

1½ teaspoons butter
¼ cup diced onion
Grated Cheddar cheese (optional)
Chopped chives for garnish (optional)

1. In a small mixing bowl, beat the eggs with the cream or milk. Season with salt and black pepper, and add the bacon to the egg mixture.
2. In a medium skillet melt the butter, tilting the skillet to coat the bottom. Sauté the onions until tender. Reduce the heat to low.
3. Add the egg mixture, stirring frequently until set. Turn the eggs onto a hot platter, top with Cheddar cheese, chives, and additional bacon, if using, and serve.

Meat Loaf

MAKES 6 SERVINGS

1½ pounds ground beef
1 egg, beaten
1 cup milk
1¼ teaspoons salt

Black pepper to taste
1 cup breadcrumbs
Gravy or tomato sauce

1. Preheat the oven to 350°F. Grease a 9 x 5-inch loaf pan and set aside.
2. In a large mixing bowl, combine the beef and egg. Pour in the milk and mix thoroughly. Add the salt, black pepper, and breadcrumbs, mixing well to combine the ingredients.
3. Shape the meat mixture into a loaf, and place it in the greased loaf pan. Bake for 1 hour, or until the meat is brown and reaches an internal temperature of 160°F. Serve with gravy or tomato sauce.

Scrambled Eggs

Desserts

COCONUT CAKE
PEACH COBBLER
FUDGE COOKIES
APPLE PIE
PEANUT BUTTER PIE
LEMON MERINGUE PIE
SUGAR COOKIES
SOUTHERN PECAN PIE
CHERRY PIE
POUND CAKE
BLUEBERRY PIE
SHOO FLY PIE
BANANA PUDDING
PEACH ICE CREAM
STRAWBERRY ICE CREAM

Coconut Cake

MAKES 8 TO 12 SERVINGS

1²/3 cups cake flour
1 cup sugar
3/4 teaspoon salt
3 teaspoons baking powder
1/3 cup plus 1 tablespoon
    shortening

1/3 cup coconut milk, room
    temperature
1/4 cup whole milk, room
    temperature
3 egg whites, room temperature
1 teaspoon vanilla extract
3 cups shredded coconut

1. Preheat the oven to 350°F. Line the bottoms of two 8-inch cake pans with parchment paper. Lightly grease the paper and sides of the pans.
2. Into a large mixing bowl, sift the cake flour. Add the sugar, salt, and baking powder, and resift 3 times. Then add the shortening and coconut milk, and beat with an electric mixer at medium speed for 2 minutes. Scrape the sides of the bowl. Stir in the whole milk, egg whites, and vanilla. Beat 2 minutes more. Scrape the sides of the bowl frequently to keep the batter smooth.
3. Pour the batter evenly into the two prepared pans, and bake for 25 minutes. Remove the cakes from the oven and let them stand for about 5 minutes. Remove them from the pans and place them on wire racks to cool thoroughly.
4. Top each layer with grated coconut, and stack the layers before serving.

Gladys loved Elvis's friends. She would greet them with her wonderful Southern hospitality. When a group of them stopped by to visit, she could be found in the kitchen cutting them a piece of freshly baked apple pie or a slice of coconut cake.

Peach Cobbler

MAKES 6 SERVINGS

Pastry for 2 piecrusts, unbaked
2 tablespoons dry white
    breadcrumbs
1 cup plus 2 tablespoons sugar,
    plus more for sprinkling
Salt to taste

1 tablespoon all-purpose flour
2 1/2 pounds peaches, peeled,
    pitted, and sliced
1 tablespoon butter, softened
1 drop almond extract
Light cream (see Note)

1. Preheat the oven to 450°F. Place the oven rack in the center of the oven.
2. Roll out 3/4 of the pastry into a 10 x 14-inch rectangle. Fold the pastry in half and gently place it in a 6 x 10-inch baking pan, unfolding the pastry (the pastry will extend over the edges of the pan). Sprinkle the breadcrumbs in the bottom of the pastry.
3. In a medium mixing bowl, combine the sugar, salt, and flour. Sprinkle 1/4 cup of the sugar mixture over the breadcrumbs.
4. Arrange the peach slices in the pastry. In a separate small bowl, stir together the butter and almond extract. Dot the peach slices with the butter mixture. Sprinkle the remaining sugar mixture over the peaches.
5. Fold the extended dough over the peaches, tucking in the corners (the center will not be covered with pastry).
6. Roll out the remaining pastry into a 3 x 7-inch rectangle. Cut a line down the center for ventilation. Place the pastry over the peaches. Brush the entire top with cream and sprinkle with sugar.
7. Bake the cobbler for 15 minutes, or until the crust begins to brown. Reduce the heat to 325° and bake for 25 minutes more. Remove the cobbler to a rack to cool. Serve with the remaining cream.

Note: If you don't have light cream, you can substitute it with a mixture of equal parts heavy cream and whole milk.

IN *THAT'S THE WAY IT IS* IN 1970

Fudge Cookies

MAKES 4 DOZEN

2 cups sifted all-purpose flour
1 1/2 teaspoons baking powder
1/4 teaspoon salt
1/2 teaspoon baking soda
1/2 cup butter
1/2 granulated sugar

1/2 cup firmly packed light brown
  sugar
2 eggs, beaten
1 teaspoon vanilla extract
2 (1-ounce) squares unsweetened
  chocolate, melted and cooled
1/4 cup buttermilk

1. Preheat the oven to 375°F. Grease a baking sheet, and set aside.
2. In a large mixing bowl, add the sifted flour, baking powder, salt, and baking soda. Sift together three times and set aside.
3. In a medium mixing bowl, cream the butter until smooth. Add the granulated sugar and brown sugar, and beat until smooth. Add the eggs and beat until fluffy. Stir in the vanilla and the cooled melted chocolate.
4. To the butter mixture beat in a third of the flour mixture, followed by half of the buttermilk. Repeat these steps until the flour mixture and buttermilk are fully incorporated into the batter, beginning and ending with the flour mixture.
5. Drop heaping teaspoonfuls of batter onto the greased baking sheet about 2 inches apart. Bake for 12 minutes. Remove the cookies from the oven and place them on a rack to cool.

Apple Pie

1 tablespoon all-purpose flour
Salt to taste
3/4 cup sugar
Pastry for 2 piecrusts, unbaked

8 medium apples, peeled and
   quartered
1 tablespoon butter
1/4 teaspoon cinnamon

1. Preheat the oven to 400°F.
2. In a large mixing bowl, blend the flour, salt, and sugar. Line a 9-inch pie pan with 1 layer of crust. Sprinkle half of the flour mixture in the bottom of the piecrust.
3. Slice the quartered apples lengthwise. Toss the apples with the remaining flour mixture. Arrange the slices close together in the bottom of the pie shell. Dot with butter. Sprinkle with cinnamon.
4. Moisten the edge of the lower crust. Top with the remaining pastry. Press down gently around the edges to seal, and trim off the excess dough. Poke the crust with a fork for ventilation, and place the pie in the oven.
5. Bake the pie for 15 minutes, then reduce the heat to 325° and continue baking for 35 minutes. The apples should be tender, with juice bubbling out of the air vents. Remove the pie to a wire rack and let it cool for 3 hours.

Peanut Butter Pie

MAKES 6–8 SERVINGS

1 cup peanut butter
1 teaspoon vanilla extract
1 1/2 cups sugar
1/2 teaspoon salt

2 eggs, well beaten
1 1/2 cups milk
Pastry for 1 piecrust, unbaked

1. Preheat the oven to 450°F.
2. In a large mixing bowl, cream together the peanut butter and vanilla. Gradually add the sugar and salt, mixing well. Add the eggs and milk, and blend thoroughly.
3. Line a 9-inch pie pan with 1 layer of crust. Turn out the filling into the piecrust, and bake for 10 minutes. Reduce the heat to 350°F and bake for 25 minutes, or until a knife inserted in the center comes out clean. Let the pie cool on a wire rack.

Apple Pie

Lemon Meringue Pie

MAKES 8 SERVINGS

1/3 cup cornstarch
13/4 cups plus 2 tablespoons sugar,
   divided
3 eggs, separated
3 tablespoons butter

11/3 tablespoons lemon zest
1/4 cup fresh lemon juice
Pastry for 1 piecrust, baked
1/4 teaspoon cream of tartar

1. Preheat the oven to 400°F.
2. In a medium saucepan mix the cornstarch and 11/2 cups of the sugar. Add 11/2 cups water and cook over medium heat, stirring constantly until thickened. Bring the mixture to a boil, and boil for 1 minute. Remove the pan from the heat.
3. In a medium mixing bowl, beat the egg yolks lightly. Pour a small amount of the hot sugar mixture into the egg yolks, stirring constantly. Add the yolk mixture to the remaining hot sugar mixture in the saucepan, stirring constantly.
4. Return the pan to the stove, and bring the mixture to a boil. Boil until thickened. Remove from the heat. Stir in the butter, lemon zest, and lemon juice. Pour the filling into the piecrust.
5. In a large mixing bowl, beat the egg whites with the cream of tartar and remaining 6 tablespoons sugar until stiff. Spread the meringue over the pie filling, making sure the meringue touches the edges of the pie. Bake for 8 minutes, or until the meringue is light brown. Let the pie cool before serving.

Elvis loved to entertain his classmates. They would sit on the grass in front of his house and listen to him sing until it was time to go in for supper.

Sugar Cookies

Sugar Cookies

MAKES 6 DOZEN

5 cups all-purpose flour
1 teaspoon baking soda
2 cups sugar, plus more for sprinkling
1 cup butter
1 cup neutral oil

2 eggs
2 teaspoons vanilla extract
1 teaspoon cream of tartar
Pinch of salt

1. In a large mixing bowl, sift the flour and baking soda. Mix in the sugar, butter, oil, eggs, vanilla extract, cream of tartar, and salt. Refrigerate the dough for 3 hours.
2. When the dough is chilled, remove it from the refrigerator and preheat the oven to 375°F.
3. Shape the dough into 1-inch balls and place the dough balls on an ungreased baking sheet. Flatten with a fork and sprinkle with sugar. Bake for about 8 minutes.

Southern Pecan Pie

MAKES 6–8 SERVINGS

Pastry for 1 piecrust, unbaked
4 eggs, lightly beaten
2/3 cup firmly packed dark brown sugar
1 1/3 cups light corn syrup
1/4 cup unsalted butter, melted

1/2 teaspoon salt
4 teaspoons all-purpose flour
2 teaspoons vanilla extract
1 1/2 cups coarsely chopped pecans

1. Preheat the oven to 400°F. Place the piecrust in a 9-inch pie pan, and bake for 10 minutes or until the crust is set but not browned. Remove the crust from the oven and set it aside. Reduce the oven temperature to 375°F.
2. In a large mixing bowl, stir together the eggs, brown sugar, corn syrup, butter, salt, flour, and vanilla. Add the pecans and mix, then pour the mixture into the partially baked pie shell.
3. Bake the pie for about 35 minutes. Cover the edges of the crust with strips of foil, if necessary, to prevent excessive browning. Cool on a wire rack, then serve.

Cherry Pie

MAKES 6–8 SERVINGS

Pastry for 2 piecrusts, unbaked
½ cup sugar
Salt to taste

3 tablespoons all-purpose flour
2½ cups canned sour red cherries
¼ teaspoon almond extract

1. Preheat the oven to 450°F. Line an 8-inch pie pan with 1 layer of crust.
2. In a large saucepan mix together the sugar, salt, and flour. Drain the juice from the cherries, reserving ¾ cup of juice. Add the cherry juice to the saucepan. Cook over medium-high heat, stirring constantly, until the mixture boils and thickens.
3. Remove the pan from the heat, and stir in the almond extract.
4. Place the cherries in the piecrust, and pour the thickened juice over the cherries.
5. Roll out the second pastry for the top crust, then cut out vents for steam. Moisten the edges of the lower crust with water, and place the top crust over the cherry filling. Press the edges together, trimming off any excess dough. Let the pie stand for 10 minutes, then flute the edges of the crust.
6. Bake for 15 minutes, or until the crust is light brown. Reduce the heat to 325°F and continue baking about 15 minutes more. Let the pie cool before serving.

IN A QUIET MOMENT AT THE PIANO

Pound Cake

MAKES 12 SERVINGS

1 cup butter, softened
1 cup sugar
¼ teaspoon lemon zest
1 teaspoon fresh lemon juice

4 eggs
2 cups cake flour
¼ teaspoon baking powder
Powdered sugar, for dusting (optional)

1. Preheat the oven to 300°F. Grease and flour a 9 x 5-inch loaf pan, and set aside.
2. In a large mixing bowl, cream together the butter and sugar. Add the lemon zest, lemon juice, and eggs. Beat well. Stir in the cake flour and baking powder, and blend until smooth.
3. Pour the batter into the loaf pan, and bake the cake for 1 hour 15 minutes. Let the cake cool before serving. Dust with powdered sugar, if using, and serve.

Blueberry Pie

MAKES 6–8 SERVINGS

1 quart fresh blueberries, washed
1 tablespoon lemon zest
1½ tablespoons fresh lemon juice
¾ cup sugar

¼ teaspoon salt
2 tablespoons all-purpose flour
Pastry for 2 piecrusts, unbaked

1. Preheat the oven to 450°F.
2. In a large mixing bowl, combine the blueberries, lemon zest, and lemon juice. Pour in the sugar, salt, and flour, and gently mix to coat the blueberries.
3. Line a pie pan with 1 layer of piecrust, and turn the blueberry mixture into the crust.
4. Moisten the rim of the bottom crust. Place the top crust over the filling and pinch the edges to seal. Make air vents in the top crust to allow steam to escape.
5. Bake the pie for about 10 minutes, then reduce the heat to 350° and bake about 30 minutes more. Let the pie cool before serving.

Pound Cake

Shoo Fly Pie

MAKES 12–16 SERVINGS

Pastry for 2 piecrusts, unbaked
1 cup molasses
1 cup warm water
1³⁄4 teaspoons baking soda, divided

2 cups all-purpose flour
1⁄4 teaspoon salt
1⁄2 cup sugar
1⁄4 cup shortening

1. Preheat the oven to 350°F. Place one piecrust each at the bottom of two 8-inch pie pans.
2. In a large mixing bowl, beat the molasses, warm water, and 1 teaspoon of the baking soda until foamy.
3. In a separate bowl combine the flour, salt, sugar, and the remaining ³⁄4 teaspoon baking soda. Cut in the shortening with a fork until the mixture resembles coarse crumbs.
4. Pour a third of the molasses mixture into the first pie pan, then pour another third into the second pie pan; reserve the last third of the molasses mixture.
5. Sprinkle a quarter of the crumb mixture over the molasses in the first pie pan, then sprinkle a quarter of the crumb mixture over the second pie. Top each pie with the remaining molasses mixture, and sprinkle with the remaining crumb mixture. Bake the pies for 45 minutes.

Banana Pudding

MAKES 4 SERVINGS

1 tablespoon unflavored gelatin
1⁄4 cup cold water
1 cup boiling water
1 cup sugar

1⁄4 cup fresh lemon juice
3 egg whites, stiffly beaten
3 bananas, peeled and sliced

1. In a small bowl soften the gelatin in the cold water for 5 minutes. Then add the boiling water and stir to dissolve. Stir in the sugar and lemon juice, and strain the mixture. Then refrigerate the mixture until somewhat thickened.
2. Whip the egg whites until frothy. Fold the beaten egg whites into the gelatin mixture.
3. Dip a 4-cup gelatin mold into cold water, then arrange the sliced bananas in the mold. Pour the gelatin mixture on top of the bananas. Refrigerate until firm, then unmold and serve.

Shoo Fly Pie

WITH PRISCILLA, LISA MARIE, AND CHARLES HODGES

Peach Ice Cream

MAKES 1 QUART

1½ cups peaches, peeled, pitted, and mashed
1¼ cups sugar, divided
1 cup milk

Salt to taste
1 tablespoon all-purpose flour
1 cup heavy cream
1 tablespoon vanilla extract

1. In a large mixing bowl, blend the peaches with 3/4 cup of the sugar, and set the mixture aside.
2. In a small saucepan heat the milk until just simmering.
3. In a separate bowl combine the remaining 1/2 cup sugar, salt, and flour. Gradually add the sugar mixture to the milk and cook over low heat, stirring constantly. Bring the mixture to a boil, and boil for 1 minute. Add the mashed peaches and stir.
4. Pour the mixture into the bowl of an ice-cream maker and freeze for about 30 minutes.
5. In a mixing bowl whip the cream until somewhat stiff. Add the vanilla. Fold the cream mixture into the frozen peaches and freeze for an additional 4 hours, stirring well after 1 hour.

Strawberry Ice Cream

1 quart ripened strawberries,
washed and hulled
1 cup sugar
1 tablespoon fresh lemon juice
1/4 teaspoon salt

1 teaspoon unflavored gelatin
1 tablespoon cold water
1 cup milk
3 cups light cream (see Note)

1. In the bowl of a large food processor, puree the strawberries to make 1 3/4 cups. Add the sugar, lemon juice, and salt, and blend. Cover the strawberry mixture and refrigerate.
2. In a small mixing bowl, soften the gelatin in cold water. Stir to dissolve.
3. In a small saucepan heat the milk until just simmering. Add the gelatin to the milk and let the mixture cool.
4. Stir in the strawberry puree and cream, and pour the mixture into the bowl of an ice-cream maker. Freeze according to the manufacturer's directions.

Note: If you don't have light cream, you can substitute it with a mixture of equal parts heavy cream and whole milk.

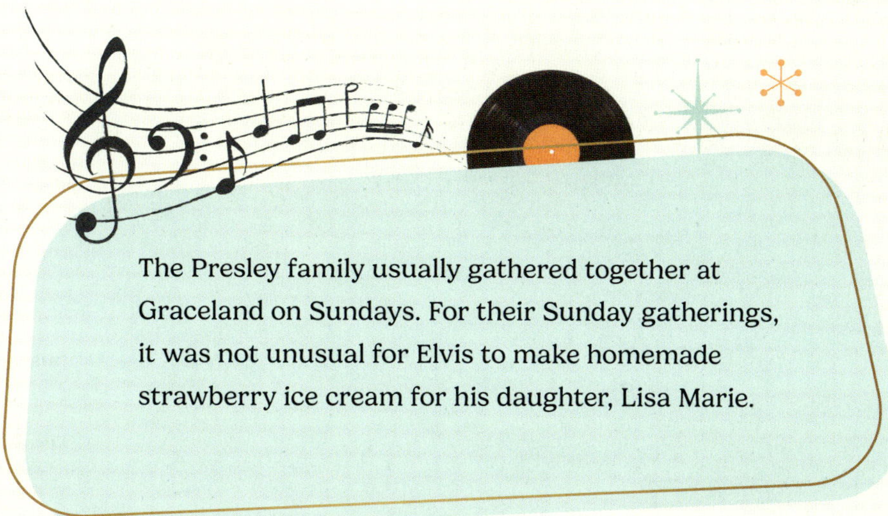

The Presley family usually gathered together at Graceland on Sundays. For their Sunday gatherings, it was not unusual for Elvis to make homemade strawberry ice cream for his daughter, Lisa Marie.

Beverages

TOMATO JUICE COCKTAIL

LEMONADE

LIMEADE

GRAPE LEMONADE

PINEAPPLE SODA

EGGNOG

CRANBERRY PUNCH

ORANGE SODA

BLACK COW

CHOCOLATE SODA

CHOCOLATE MALTED SHAKE

HOT CARAMEL MILK SHAKE

Tomato Juice Cocktail

Tomato Juice Cocktail

MAKES 5 SERVINGS

2½ cups tomato juice
1½ teaspoons finely chopped onion
1 teaspoon sugar

2 teaspoons fresh lemon juice
¼ teaspoon salt
¼ teaspoon Worcestershire sauce

1. In a blender mix the tomato juice, onion, sugar, lemon juice, salt, and Worcestershire sauce until well combined.
2. Strain the mixture and pour into a pitcher. Refrigerate until very chilled.

Lemonade

MAKES 4 SERVINGS

4 lemons, divided
½ cup sugar

16 large ice cubes, crushed
Mint for garnish

1. Cut the lemons in half. From one of the lemon halves, slice 4 thin slices and set aside.
2. Into a small pitcher squeeze the remaining lemons—you should have about ½ cup fresh lemon juice. Remove the seeds from the juice but do not strain. Add the sugar and crushed ice. Stir until the sugar dissolves and the ice is almost melted.
3. Garnish four glasses with the reserved lemon slices and mint. Serve immediately.

DRIVING THROUGH MEMPHIS

SHOWING HIS TALENTS ON THE DRUMS

Limeade

10 limes, divided
3/4 cup sugar
2 cups ice water

1/2 teaspoon grated lime zest
Mint for garnish (optional)

1. Into a small pitcher squeeze 9 of the limes. Remove any seeds, but do not strain the juice. Thinly slice the remaining lime, and set aside.
2. In the pitcher combine the lime juice, sugar, water, and lime zest. Mix well.
3. Fill five glasses 1/3 full with crushed ice. Add the limeade. Garnish each with a lime slice and mint sprig, if using.

Grape Lemonade

MAKES 5 SERVINGS

1/2 cup fresh lemon juice, seeds
  removed
3/4 cup fresh orange juice, seeds
  removed
1/4 cup sugar

1 1/4 cups grape juice, chilled
1 3/4 cups ice water
Lemon slices for garnish
Mint for garnish

1. To a small pitcher add the lemon and orange juices. Stir in the sugar until thoroughly dissolved. Add the chilled grape juice and ice water.
2. Place 2 tablespoons crushed ice cubes into 5 small glasses. Fill with lemonade. Garnish each with a lemon slice and a mint sprig.

Pineapple Soda

MAKES 1 SERVING

2 tablespoons crushed pineapple
1 tablespoon sugar
Salt to taste

1 teaspoon milk
1/2 cup carbonated water
1 scoop vanilla ice cream

1. In a 10-ounce glass combine the crushed pineapple, sugar, salt, and milk. Stir thoroughly.
2. Add 1/4 cup of the carbonated water and the ice cream. Stir a few times to blend.
3. Add the remaining 1/4 cup carbonated water.

Limeade

Eggnog

MAKES 6 SERVINGS

2 eggs
1/4 cup sugar
Salt to taste
2 cups milk

1 tablespoon rum extract
1/2 cup cream, stiffly beaten
Fresh ground nutmeg

1. In the top of a double boiler, beat the eggs, sugar, and salt. Stir in the milk.
2. Add 2 inches of water to the bottom of the double boiler and bring to a simmer. Place the pan with the egg mixture over the simmering water of the double boiler, and stir frequently until heated through, then chill.
3. Stir in the rum extract, then fold in the stiffly beaten cream and add a dash of nutmeg. Serve immediately.

Cranberry Punch

MAKES 2 1/2 QUARTS

1 quart fresh cranberries
1 cup sugar
5 whole cloves
1/2 teaspoon lemon zest

1/2 teaspoon orange zest
2 tablespoons fresh lemon juice
1 quart apple juice, chilled
1 medium orange, sliced for garnish

1. In a large saucepan bring 4 cups of water to a boil. Add the cranberries, cover, and boil until the skins pop.
2. Into a large, heatproof bowl, strain the mixture. Push the cranberries through the sieve to get as much flavor from them as possible.
3. In a large mixing bowl, combine the strained cranberries, sugar, cloves, lemon zest, and orange zest. Cover and refrigerate until chilled.
4. Add the lemon juice and apple juice, and stir to blend. Remove the cloves before serving. Garnish with orange slices.

Eggnog

Orange Soda

Orange Soda

MAKES 1 SERVING

1 tablespoon orange zest
1/4 cup fresh orange juice
1 teaspoon fresh lemon juice
1 tablespoon sugar

1 teaspoon milk
1/2 cup lime seltzer water, divided
1 large scoop vanilla ice cream
Orange slices for garnish

1. In a 10-ounce glass combine the orange zest and juice, lemon juice, sugar, and milk.
2. Add 1/4 cup lime seltzer water and the ice cream. Mix slightly.
3. Add the remaining 1/4 cup lime seltzer water, garnish with an orange slice, and serve immediately.

Black Cow

MAKES 4 SERVINGS

4 cups root beer, divided
4 teaspoons milk

4 large scoops vanilla ice cream

1. In each of 4 glasses about 10 ounces each, combine 1/4 cup root beer and 1 teaspoon milk. Add a scoop of ice cream to each glass and stir slightly.
2. Divide the remaining 3 cups root beer among the glasses, and serve.

Chocolate Soda

MAKES 1 SERVING

2 tablespoons chocolate syrup
1 teaspoon milk
1/2 cup carbonated water, divided

1 large scoop vanilla or chocolate ice cream

1. Place the chocolate syrup in a 10-ounce glass. Add the milk and 1/4 cup of the carbonated water. Stir.
2. Add the ice cream and the remaining 1/4 cup carbonated water.

Chocolate Malted Shake

MAKES 2 SERVINGS

½ cup chocolate syrup, chilled
¼ cup malted milk powder
2 cups milk

1 large scoop vanilla or chocolate
   ice cream
Salt to taste

1. In a blender combine the chocolate syrup, malted milk powder, milk, ice cream, and salt.
2. Blend thoroughly until frothy. Pour into serving glasses.

Hot Caramel Milk Shake

MAKES 1 SERVING

1 egg yolk
1 tablespoon caramel syrup
Salt to taste

1 cup hot milk
¼ teaspoon vanilla extract

1. In the top of a double boiler beat the egg yolk until thick. Add the caramel syrup, salt, and milk.
2. Add 2 inches of water to the bottom of the double boiler and bring to a simmer. Place the pan with the egg and caramel mixture over the simmering water of the double boiler, and heat until just simmering. Remove the pan from the heat.
3. Add the vanilla and beat until frothy. Serve immediately.

Elvis's friends and family knew that he drank a lot of milk, water, and soda pop. On certain occasions, he preferred chocolate milk.

Chocolate Malted Shake

Acknowledgments

When one thinks about Elvis Presley, one doesn't necessarily think about cooking or, for that matter, a cookbook. We didn't either at first. The concept for this cookbook came about when we thought about Elvis Presley and where he chose to live.

But undertaking this book involved more than we anticipated, and we would like to thank the many people who helped us through the project: Harriet Stockanes, our permissions editor, who got the ball rolling for us; C. Barry Ward, attorney for the Presley Estate, who gave us the final go-ahead; Jaques Dulin, whose patience and confidence in us was never less than 100 percent; Irene Maleti, president of the King of Our Hearts Elvis Presley Fan Club, and her husband, Sam, for pointing us in the right direction; a very special thank-you to Linda Everett, who opened her photo albums of Elvis and shared the many treasures hidden inside; Alvena Roy, for sharing her recipes and memories of Elvis; and Carol and Trudy, for getting us past the finish line.

We would also like to thank our many friends who encouraged us every step of the way, especially Anne, who gave us the idea for the title;

and Jon, for his patience during those many late-night phone calls about the manuscript and his help with the index; Bernie, Lewis, Charlie, and Debbie, who were there from the beginning; Richard, Margaret, Dorre, and Meiko, who stood by with support during the many months of editing and rewriting.

And the greatest thank-you to our families, especially Ronnie and Bonnie, for their special loving, listening, and support; Treva and Joretta, for their unconditional support; Stephen, Kathy, and Mike, for being the best a sister could ever have; a big thank-you to Madeleine and Molly, who have been extremely good to us the past two years; and to our parents, who taught us to take a chance and gave us the support and love to do so.

A special thank-you to Ron Pitkin; his wife, Julie; and Larry Stone at Rutledge Hill Press for their patience and helpful guidance in getting this book off the ground and for believing in our idea from the start.

And finally to Elvis, for giving us more than thirty years of magic. And to his many fans, who continue to keep that magic alive.

—Thanks to you all!

Glossary of Cooking Terms

Bake: To cook covered or uncovered in an oven.

Baste: To moisten foods during cooking with pan drippings or special sauce to add flavor and to prevent drying.

Beat: To make a mixture smooth by adding air through a brisk whipping or stirring motion using a spoon or electric mixer.

Blend: To thoroughly mix two or more ingredients until smooth and uniform.

Boil: To cook a liquid at boiling temperature where bubbles rise to the surface and break. For a full rolling boil, bubbles form rapidly throughout the mixture.

Braise: To cook slowly with a small amount of liquid in a tightly covered pan on top of a stove or in an oven.

Broil: To cook by direct heat, usually in a broiler or over coals.

Chill: To place in a refrigerator to reduce the temperature.

Chop: To cut into pieces the size of peas with a knife, chopper, or blender.

Cool: To remove from heat and let stand at room temperature.

Cream: To beat with a spoon or electric mixer until the mixture is soft and smooth. When applied to blending shortening or butter and sugar, the mixture is beaten until light and fluffy.

Cut in: To mix shortening or butter with dry ingredients using a pastry blender or knives.

Dice: To cut food into small cubes or in uniform size and shape.

Dissolve: To blend a dry substance in a liquid to form a solution.

Glaze: A mixture applied to food that hardens or becomes firm and adds flavor and a glossy appearance.

Grate: To rub a grater that separates the food into very fine particles.

Julienne: To cut into long, thin strips.

Marinate: To allow food to stand in a liquid to tenderize and to enhance flavor.

Mince: To cut or finely chop food into very small pieces.

Parboil: To cook partially by boiling for a brief period.

Poach: To cook in hot liquid, being careful that the food holds its shape during the cooking process.

Precook: To cook food partially or completely before final cooking or reheating.

Roast: To cook uncovered with water added, usually in an oven.

Sauté: To brown or cook in a small amount of butter or oil.

Scald: To bring a liquid to just below the boiling point.

Scallop: To bake foods in a casserole dish with sauce or other liquid.

Sear: To char, scorch, or burn the surface.

Steam: To cook in steam with or without pressure. A small amount of water is used.

Stir: To mix ingredients with a circular motion until well blended.

Toss: To mix ingredients lightly.

Whip: To beat rapidly to incorporate air and produce expansion.

Photography Credits